CYCLES OF CAPITALISM

THE AGE OF NON-LINEARITY
OF OUTCOMES

ASHKAN HAMZEHI

Cycles of Capitalism
Copyright © 2023 by Ashkan Hamzehi

All rights reserved. No part of this publication may be reproduced, distributed, or transmitted in any form or by any means, including photocopying, recording, or other electronic or mechanical methods, without the prior written permission of the author, except in the case of brief quotations embodied in critical reviews and certain other non-commercial uses permitted by copyright law.

Tellwell Talent
www.tellwell.ca

ISBN
978-1-77941-072-6 (Hardcover)
978-1-77941-071-9 (Paperback)
978-1-77941-073-3 (eBook)

Table of Contents

Chapter 1 The Notion of Inherent Cyclicality 1

Chapter 2 Cycles in a Historical Context 8

Chapter 3 The Strongest Force in the Universe 34

Chapter 4 Market Psychology 49

Chapter 5 Stages of Capitalism 56

Chapter 6 Navigating into the Future and Solutions 72

References 75

Thanks to cold and long winter nights in Alberta that induce thought formation.

Chapter One

The Notion of Inherent Cyclicality

Thanks to the long winter nights of the Canadian prairies, I have had plenty of time to search for an understanding about how humans behave regarding financial decisions. I have always searched to understand self not as an isolated entity but as a part of a much bigger paradigm called culture and ideology, which define us all around the world. I admit that I have also experienced a dopamine surge through the years when searching for this answer. In this book, I try to explain how capitalism has shaped all eight billion people on planet Earth, causing them to behave and act in a certain manner in this vast picture of trade, speculation, war, and collaboration. I also explain why I believe that capitalism has already reached its global climax and is in decline due to the recognition of its inherent deficiencies.

I, along with the rest of the world, am observing global turmoil but with an understanding of the reason behind each event. These global challenges include a wide array of difficulties and deficiencies in our societies that can't be ignored, including poverty, the opioid crisis, homelessness, record suicide numbers, and an unprecedented division between the haves and have nots.

I'm not mad at anybody or any entity. I am in peace with it all as it unravels. Hopefully, by the end of this book you'll understand the reasons behind these global tensions and that our behaviour, societies, and future prospects are, to a great degree, the result of the core ideology of capitalism and compound interest. We need to understand this paradigm through an economic, psychological, social, mathematical, and historical perspective in order to know our world, as well as ourselves. This book might help the fish to understand the fish bowl, as the fish has been experiencing nothing else while submerged in the bowl. After this, maybe we can get into the ocean together.

For the first time in the history of humanity, capitalism is the sole and dominant force in every country around the world, so it can create more severe fluctuations in the markets and affect more people. Even former communist countries like China and Russia have fully embraced capitalism in recent decades; as a matter of fact, communist China is amongst the most prominent capitalist countries of today.

I believe that capitalism has tremendous influence in our world. It's the paradigm and frame that holds together and shapes the global human consciousness around trade, consumption, competition, and collaboration. Compound growth has also been a strong force behind the rise and fall of almost every culture in the history of civilization. Hopefully after reading the next few chapters, you will fully understand this notion at its heart.

What is this force that has impacted our history? Can it be separated from humans? Can we eventually attain a different global consciousness, separate from capitalism? To answer these questions, we need to understand the basics of exponential functions and compound growth that have affected us over the past five thousand years of our civilized history. I have been privileged to study different civilizations over these years in which we view the manifestation of global consciousness in distinguished forms. Having said that, we don't need to go far back in time to fully understand the cycles of capitalism. The twentieth century provides us with sufficient data to fully grasp the range of possibilities that can happen again in our lifetime.

Capitalism is inherently cyclical due to the mathematical equation of compounding and exponential functions, so it's predisposed to boom-and-bust cycles. Market cycles can be divided into short- and long-term cycles of typically eight, thirty, and eighty years in length, and the timeframes can also change due to different underlying factors. Understanding these cycles, stages of capitalism, and the maturity of the economy is very important, since depending on the maturity of the cycle, economic outcomes can be paradoxical or even opposing.

John Maynard Keynes famously said, "In the long run, we are all dead." I believe it's a profoundly philosophical admission regarding the cyclical nature of capitalism. It's also a recognition of the fact that all cycles of capitalism die off, regardless of how consequential it can be for billions of people.

Markets always achieve equilibrium naturally, but it can come at the high cost of an abrupt end to a cycle. The common belief amongst the elite is that authorities should interfere in the markets to prevent markets from seeking natural equilibrium, and unintentionally, they raise the accumulated stress in the markets in the long run until a major event happens. The more diverted the market is from the equilibrium, the more painful the return to equilibrium becomes for billions of people around the world.

The cyclical nature of markets manifests itself differently in different sectors of the economy through time. We also tend to explain significant historical events with an innocent naïveté and simplicity, which results in losing out on those lessons and not learning from the past. For example, if somebody asks why did WWII start, the answer can be as simple as there was a rise of evil. We forget about the economic cycles of the 1930s that resulted in rise of evil.

In order to understand the markets, one has to abandon common sense. Humankind is prone to understand every phenomenon in a linear fashion, since we have evolved in a world of linear equations. Markets act under a different mathematical equation; financial markets are all about non-linearity, compounding, volatility, fluctuations, and complexity. For the purposes of this book, I encourage the reader to start viewing the world in a non-linear and random fashion, and please acknowledge that certainty of outcome can only be expressed based on randomness, probability, and accepting the concept of fallibility through every endeavour in life.

In order to understand financial markets, one needs to understand the oceanic economic tides and huge up-and-down swings of the markets.

Capitalism Is Manic-Depressive

Debt and leverage always magnify these swings. In a funny way, they have the same effect as serving alcohol at parties: there are always a few people at the party who overindulge, and then there's some sort of hangover the next day. Debt basically enables you to consume tomorrow's consumption today, knowing that tomorrow you have to work harder to pay for the past. Furthermore, incomes can disappear, but debt always stays. Although debt and leverage provide the consumer with a boost of consumption for a while, it also can harm the consumer when the credit window shuts down exactly like how the game of musical chairs is played.

The markets that carry a greater level of leverage are more susceptible to bigger and more volatile downturns. In a sense, smaller and less sophisticated markets that carry smaller amounts of leverage might tolerate the economic downturns with less pain compared to the highly-levered and capital-intensive developed economies. That's why emerging markets that carry less debt and leverage might have a better opportunity as well as an easier task of dealing with global challenges, including debt overhang, supply chain disruptions, and disruptions in trade.

Global economic shocks affect all the regions in the world; however, corporations, governments, and households that are expensive to run and need more capital to function on a daily basis can feel the squeeze in a harder way.

Markets also exhibit a manic-depressive psychology due to repetitive cycles of fear and greed that are exaggerated by financial leverage. To understand the bipolar behaviour of the markets, you can observe the severe fluctuations of different assets over the last decade, going from extreme fear and sell-off to a euphoric buy, sending the prices to the moon. With each new high in prices, some asset owners develop a fanatic belief in their holdings, as if it's their religion, and they forget that investment is nothing more than the logical allocation of resources into different assets in a diversified manner.

Market participants tend to allocate more and more resources into their current positions, only to face an impeding fall when market sentiment shifts from one extreme to the other. Due to concept of reflexivity in the markets, each downturn encourages a self-fulfilling prophecy of absolute fear of selling, and each upturn creates a self-reinforcing irrational exuberance to buy.

Financial markets usually act opposite to the simple economic laws of supply and demand. It's wise to say that financial markets no longer abide by the early economic laws Adam Smith introduced. The baker and the butcher have turned into speculators in the age of modern finance.

The self-reinforcing cycle of panic amongst the market players is always irrational and carries disastrous consequences. Abruptly, markets run out of buyers, and the selling frenzy starts. It's almost like when all the elephants in a circus panic and run for the exit door all at the same time, only to tear down the whole circus.

If you're a pessimistic person, you might even argue that capitalism always offers a boom and doom scenario, since it has to exponentially grow to the end of time. One time I heard an activist compare the endless compound growth of capitalism to the ideology of a cancer cell that can lead to our extinction. I reluctantly enjoy reading articles like that due to their sense of needed awareness.

I always hope and pray that capitalism doesn't bring down the system through an ugly deleveraging. The fully desired outcome is a beautiful deleveraging that resets the system without too much pain. That's why these cycles are so important in order to have a harmless deleveraging so that the system can grow again. Having said that, history has shown that sometimes when you have bubbles everywhere, it can turn into fires everywhere. The largest and most destructive downturns usually happen after decades of financial innovations to smoothen these cycles. By smoothening these cycles for decades, you do nothing short of accumulating more stress and complexity in the system until you end up with a systemic shock. I tend to believe that we're getting closer to such event, if it hasn't already happened. This was one of the reasons I decided to write this book, in order to raise awareness.

For example, if a large East Asian country like China grows in double digits for decades, using all kinds of financial innovations, it can't afford to go to single digits of growth without an implosion, so smoothening the cycles for decades via financial stimuli only defers the inevitable. No economic innovation can turn lead into gold, so this is no different. No matter how many ghost towns you build, the only option for that highly-levered economy is to cherish authoritarianism as the only means to survive for decades to come. What China achieved in thirty years was the equivalent of what the United States achieved in 250 years, but only to realize that you can't compound and grow in double digits and then go to single digits without a massive event. Centralized rule in East Asia is not the choice anymore, but it's the only way to establish law and order instead of chaos and anarchy.

I have a few libertarian friends in Alberta whom I love and admire; I would like to consider myself a libertarian at heart, but I also believe that true liberty is the fruit of a prosperous economy. Forgive me for my perhaps rude sincerity, but I believe asking for democratic rights when capitalism has reached its down cycle is no longer a valid inquiry. There's an old saying in the Middle East that says in times of crisis, a powerful ruler who can maintain law and order is better than a democratic one who loses his grip on power, brings disorder to the public, and invites foreign invasion. I believe the wiser notion is to recognize the dire challenges that our governments face and to support them.

Democracies flourish when the underlying economy enables them to do so; WE THE PEOPLE was only achieved in history due to the economic prosperity of the new colonies in America. Demanding more and more democratic rights in times of severe economic deleveraging is a tough and unattainable task. You have no rights until a prosperous economy lets you afford your rights, especially when it comes to health care and pensions around the world. Your democratic choices are non-existent when the compound growth reaches a T-junction or, God forbid, a cement wall. In times of economic crisis, citizens can be politically and socially active, which is great, but in reality, they have to pick their poison between totalitarianism and chaotic anarchy. I even have a deeper philosophical debate regarding mutual inclusivity of capitalism and democracy. It can be said that every market player is the natural enemy of free markets because every market player is seeking domination in the markets via competitive means of business, so it is always a daunting task to provide every citizen with equal democratic rights especially when it comes to competing with giant international conglomerates.

The decline of democratic values is evident all around the world due to economic hardship caused by debt saturation, social inequality, trade imbalances, and lack of productivity. At this moment, all the significant economies of the world are dealing with the same challenges, and our only hope is a peaceful global financial reset and a restoration of fair trade amongst nations; otherwise, the twenty-first century might become the era of protectionism as well as totalitarian policies that results in the erosion of our beloved democratic values that took us centuries to achieve.

The twenty-first century could become the century of endarkenment unless we turn it into the continuation of enlightenment all around the world by understanding the causes of our troubles and solving these core and structural issues. Debt restructuring, which is desperately needed everywhere, is a massive challenge, since everybody's debt is somebody else's asset, but it's our main hope to prevent an era of global endarkenment.

Having said that, painful five-to-eight-year economic downturns should have been fully allowed to happen in order to prevent a systemic shock. A five-year downturn is similar to a painful rehab for an alcoholic to get healthy, but only so that he or she can go back to streets and party again. Our main mistake has been to prevent these cycles from happening over the last three or four decades, so we have to face a much bigger challenge now globally. The drunk mature economies of the world have no choice but to go through a very painful rehab after forty years of accumulating debt, leverage, trade imbalances, financial stimuli, and speculation.

Let's view the past economic cycles in the next chapter. The best advice is to stay away from bubbles, since both pessimists and optimists are right regarding bubbles. The optimist is right when the price rises; the pessimist is right when the bubbles burst. At the end, there is zero net gain for either of them, so bubbles always create zero net gain for societies in aggregate.

Chapter Two

Cycles in a Historical Context

Tulip Mania

Economic cycles have always occurred. Everybody has heard of the Dutch tulip mania of 1634–1637, when the price of one tulip bulb was equal to the price of a house at its manic peak. Some years ago when I read about tulip mania, I thought this phenomenon would never happen again, due to the advancement of technology, connectivity, and the better understanding amongst market players. Then I observed crypto mania in recent years firsthand.

Mississippi Bubble

In 1716, John Law, one of the pioneers of financial engineering, started a new paradigm in finance. Earlier in his life, he'd been accused of murdering a man in a duel. He also was a gambler who believed in new mathematic laws that governed randomness. He designed the so-called Mississippi bubble. First, he established a fiat monetary base that was the legal tender for government tax payments. Second, he established a fractional reserve mechanism based on available gold, silver, and land. Third, he built the Mississippi company to collateralize its shares against the government debt.

The shares of the company soared to extreme levels, like any other speculative bubble that's supported by the government, only to realize an abrupt and impending fall a few years later. In order to contain the self-reinforcing down cycle, John Law had to devalue the fiat currency, which ended in a hyper-inflationary crisis all around France. Riots erupted, and he had to flee the country in order to save his life, while leaving all his possessions behind in France.

A few years ago, there was a heated debate about this new concept called the "modern monetary theory." I knew there was nothing new or modern about it, since John Law had tried it in 1716 in a similar format. Modern monetary theory is correct as a theory, but it never works for an import-driven economy. If you have an open economy that imports goods and sells those imported items as its own GDP, you can't implement modern monetary theory unless the country that exports the goods agrees to it. If you dilute the value of your currency via modern monetary theory, you can end up in a situation where your trade partners won't buy your government bonds anymore and will gradually decouple. Under this circumstance, the modern monetary theory results in hyperinflation.

South Sea Bubble

The South Sea bubble of 1720 brings to mind another John—John Blunt.

The initial confidence in the South Sea shares was due to the full-fledged support of the king, so the notion was that nothing could go wrong if the government was fully behind an entity. There was also an element of optimism that the South Sea Company was going to pioneer a new era of trade.

John Blunt enabled the ongoing buying frenzy by fully implementing the concept of buying shares based on margin. They could reduce the margin requirements each time the market needed more liquidity in order to support the irrational price of the shares. Of course, the laws of gravity set by Isaac Newton exist even in the financial markets, and prices can't go straight to the moon. Soon people realized that the current share prices couldn't be justified, and the panic to sell resulted in the evaporation of the majority of the company's assets.

The interesting point of the story is that Issac Newton himself forgot about the laws of gravity and became the victim of the scheme. Initially, he witnessed all his friends getting rich by buying South Sea shares, and of course nothing is more painful than watching your neighbours and friends get rich while you stay poor, so he couldn't resist the urge to jump in with both feet when the price was at its peak, so he put most of his retirement savings into the shares only to realize a total loss later on. He allegedly but famously said that he could calculate the motion of heavenly bodies but not the madness of people.

These days, we have companies with extremely high price-earnings ratios that are reminiscent of the South Sea bubble. The investors believe that the company is going to bring a new era of trade and technology to the world without paying much attention to the actual annual earnings. Even now as I write this book, the heads of some of these companies, who are also charismatic figures, always try to pull out new publicity stunts to keep the flow of the new investors coming. But then one day, the magician runs out of rabbits to pull out of his sleeves, and the scheme runs out of the positive net investors. At that point, every market player realizes that price-earnings ratios matter. It's too late by that time, since there is no late remedy for stupidity and insanity of the herd.

In markets, the act of decision-making is removed from the individual and transferred to the aggregate behaviour of the herd. This psychological phenomenon can further intensify the boom-and-bust cycles, especially when you add debt, leverage, and margin investing to the equation.

Roaring Twenties and The Great Depression

The Roaring Twenties was another one of these interesting cycles. After World War I, there was a sense of optimism that the troubles belonged to the past, and the era of eternal prosperity was ahead. For the first time, Americans could consume and buy products using credit cards and pay for it later. Industries were growing, so there were a lot of new consumer products, including housewares, kitchen appliances, and automobiles. The advertisement industry also took off via all the celebrities to promote more domestic consumption.

The 1920s were unique years due to a rivalry between traditional values and modernity. The consumerism of the 1920s had to fight the frugal values of the American family of the nineteenth century. Let's not forget that the United States experienced its leap of growth and prosperity during the gilded age between 1877 and 1900, which was a conservative era, so in the 1920s, society deviated from those values toward a new paradigm called modernity.

Women also joined the work force and went to colleges in great numbers; they also successfully earned the right to vote. Before that, a man used to vote for the family unit, but society was moving toward individualism and needed a one person/one vote system. Women also could express themselves more freely; for example, in the 1920s, there was a rise of a phenomenon called flappers. They were a subculture of young women who expressed themselves differently than what was traditionally expected of them at the time. Flappers wore short skirts, drank alcohol, smoked cigarettes, had casual sex, and drove automobiles. At the same time, in contrast, some cities, like Chicago, implemented beach police to check and control women's attire at the beach so that it didn't conflict with the traditionally accepted norms of society.

The 1920s saw the initiation of multiculturalism due to the need for foreign workers in the new industries. Immigration was also an element of modernity that was rejected by the traditionalists.

The prohibition of alcohol was in place by law, which was a hard-line decision; however, it wasn't strictly enforced by the fraction of society who sought modernity. The same could be said regarding gambling laws and their enforcement. Living in Halifax as a student in early 2000s, I visited a few museums that demonstrated how Canadians used to smuggle rum into the United States back in the old days, and I had my fair share of now-legal rum cake. The cake is also topped with coconut and pecans, which makes it more tasteful and also the subject of intense cravings.

Leaving the rum cakes behind, the Roaring Twenties enhanced the livelihood of a great fraction of society, especially the big-city dwellers; however, it didn't bring prosperity to everybody with the same speed and velocity; some form of social fragmentation and jealousy existed amongst the different classes. In some cases, it resulted in resentment and the popularity of extremist organizations that gathered momentum around the concept of race. I don't like to write about it in this book, since it can create intense emotions and be a sensitive topic for the reader. The left-behind people resented the elevated people by cherishing extremism and supremacy. One of the most consequential problems with capitalism is social inequality, which is inherent in the system. We can sense the same resentment from the people of the central "fly over states" toward the rich controllers of industry and capital to this day.

In general, the American family moved away from the traditional values and accepted the norms of the time, evolving to match the requirements of the modern era in which consumption, materialism, and physical prosperity were the important elements. Common sense holds that societies always evolve, and modernity is the inevitable outcome. Resisting change is the fool's game; however, diverting from traditions through drastic social engineering in a short amount of time can be severely consequential, as well as risky, for the general public. Unique traditions and rituals that existed for centuries or even millennia can't be deemed trivial via a metaphysical approach and be abandoned quickly. That's why the conflict between modernity and traditionalism is preordained and eternal.

In 1920s, laissez-faire economic policies were the dominant and accepted notion amongst the leaders and politicians. There were many cultural and scientific breakthroughs in the Roaring Twenties, including the formation and growth of jazz music, progress in the automobile industry, and the illumination of the cities.

The Roaring Twenties is the poster child for the self-reinforcing cyclical behaviour of the markets and swift turns between excessive greed and fear amongst the market participants. During that decade, the market players could purchase stock shares based on margin, so they only needed to put down 10 per cent cash, and the margin or associated loan covered the rest of the required funds to purchase the stock. Buying stocks on margin was very profitable for both the market participants and the banks, so it created its own self-reinforcing cycle to buy more and more. At some point, 40 per cent of all bank loans were issued only to buy stocks. The market got so hot that almost every shoeshine boy on Wall Street was suggesting their favourite stock picks to their clients.

Of course, like any other cycle, on October 29, 1929, the fear of loss prevailed, and fear is always a greater force than greed, so it acts very quickly to wipe out a huge portion of presumed wealth of the nation. The stock market collapse of 1929 resulted in the Great Depression, protectionism, and possibly contributed to the Second World War, which became the darkest moment in the history of humanity.

Japanese Bubble in the 1980s

In the 1980s, the dominant themes were globalization, removing capital controls, collaboration, free trade, and creating the new global village. Romanticism over global relations made everybody drunk on love for free trade. It was thought to be a win/win situation—the rich get richer, prosperity trickles down, the poor get richer, and all the countries prosper and abide by international laws, forever in peace and prosperity. That era was full of liberating ideas about reviving the economic model through less regulation and more reliance on free markets. It can be called the era of free market fanaticism.

Today we can view the history from our rearview mirror and easily judge them as being naive; however, in the 1980s, that naïveté was natural and well-fitted to its time, fashion, and music. Let's not forget the '80s hair.

Japan was also opening up to the world and had a great trade surplus with its trading partners. Japan wanted to transform itself into a more Westernized and open economy in order to bring a higher quality of life to its citizens. In the 1980s, the Bank of Japan significantly increased the window guidance loan quotas in order to boost growth, but when the banks ran out of credit-worthy clients, they had to lend to risky businesses in order to fulfill the quotas. Loans grew in double digits in 1980s and consequently created a surplus of cash and buying power. Newly created liquidity flew to the stock market and the real estate market in great magnitude. In five years' time, Japan had roughly around 250 per cent growth in both the real estate and stock markets.

The Japanese also went on a shopping spree and bought many valuable assets around the world.

At the peak of the bubble, the madness of the markets reached an unbelievable point, and the Imperial Gardens that surrounded the Imperial

Palace in Tokyo were worth as much as the entire state of California. The general mood of the people was one of confidence, exuberance, and partying. On the streets of Tokyo, even waving a $100 bill couldn't capture a cab driver's attention.

A businessman could wake up and get a call from his banker to go to the bank, sign a few papers, get a loan, and buy a property, knowing that the property would double in value in a short time. He could flip the property in one year and make a significant gain. Many automobile companies had bigger profits speculating in the markets rather than making cars. Price to earnings ratios also increased to an astonishing number, sixty-five, which was very alarming although didn't garner much attention at the time.

Of course, everybody is happy during the boom, since there's a tremendous sense of wealth creation through the rise of asset prices; the tax base goes up for the municipalities as well as the governments, and banks are happy to issue more loans. The central bank is incentivized to avoid being the party pooper by pricking the bubble, which doesn't do anything but stall economic growth.

Like any other bubble, at some point that markets run out of the new investors, exponential credit growth dries up, and compound growth stalls. As with other crashes, no injury is incurred by the extreme speed and velocity until the market reaches an abrupt and sudden stop. In 1990, the Japanese stock market dropped by 32 per cent. Soon after, greed turned into fear, and financial institutions stopped lending adequately. Five million Japanese people lost their jobs. The stock market continued its devaluation well into the new millennium, only to recover in 2021 after three decades. Japan today is still not at the level and magnitude of the Japan of the 1980s.

Land prices also continued their decline in the following decades by up to 80 per cent at some point. Many Japanese companies found themselves in balance sheet recession and no longer willing to borrow.

Although Japan has an ancient culture with amazingly talented people, it lost three decades after the crash of 1990, during which the number of social diseases rose and suicides went up, even amongst children. Japan ended up with other social problems, like the hikikomori phenomenon. A Hikikomori is a person who wisely realizes that their economic contributions to society aren't going to be well reimbursed, so they stop their social endeavours totally.

The Japanese also suffer from hyper-individualism and a lack of adequate human connectivity that has led to further depression in their demographics. Every year, many reclusive people die in Japan, and nobody gets notified for days or weeks until neighbours notify the authorities. Hyper-individualism can be due to the fact that at the end stages of the economic cycle, the cost of human interactions gets very high. The elderly are often left alone, since they can't financially afford to play their traditional role as a provider for their grandchildren; for example, a lonely Japanese grandfather can't invite his grandchildren out and pay for their lunch, so he chooses the companionship of his dog as a more economically feasible option.

Japan also has severe demographic issues, since young Japanese don't date and procreate sufficiently anymore. This reminds us that economic cycles can have enormous social and psychological consequences on millions of people and can last for decades.

I have always been aware of social challenges that existed in Japan for the past few decades, but I recently realized that those social features are coming to my beloved Canada, especially after the COVID pandemic. This includes the reduction of human connectivity through concerts, parties, family reunions, travels, and meeting colleagues at work. More and more people work from home and lose the companionship of their coworkers. More and more students study from home and miss the joy of meeting their classmates. It's also becoming more common for younger Canadians to live in their parents' basements as a Hikikomori and play video games most of the time, so Japan might be a good guide to predict our deflationary destiny in the future. Some argue that the chances for Japanification of many economies around the world are high. In contrast, my main concern is that we'll be Argentinized by super inflation. When end stage capitalism approaches, you have to either go Japanese or the Argentinian way.

Although Japan is a modern society with peaceful and cultured citizens, it's in no way, shape, or form comparable to Japan in the 1980s in terms of global impact, output, and happiness of the citizens.

Dot-com Bubble

The dot-com bubble of the late 1990s serves as an informative case study. As with other bubbles, in the late 1990s, there was a great sense of optimism that the internet was going to revolutionize the world; bubbles usually form when market confidence, market conditions, and economic growth are perceived to be at perfect levels. After the economic boom of the 1990s, confidence in the markets reached its climax; therefore, the price of every dot-com company was expected to go through the roof. This was a false premise. At that time, I was a young boy living in Toronto, Canada. One day we had to call a handyman to repair our dishwasher. Within minutes, he started bragging about his investments in dot-com companies and the fact that soon he would retire on that wealth, as said the guy who stood at the hot dog stand on the block. There was this overall belief that the old laws of economics were no longer in place, and we were in a new era of prosperity and great moderation. New internet companies formed and sold shares without proving their established annual earnings.

As long as you could sell a story, the market bought it, even if there was no substance behind the story. Businesses didn't need to show their revenue to sell shares; they could sell shares based on how many pages they served on the web, or the number of clicks on the internet. Price to earnings ratios reached thirty-five, but some companies reached price to earnings ratios of above four hundred, and no evaluation could be justified in a logical sense.

In addition, there was a huge formation of new credit in terms of mortgages, loans, and credit cards that facilitated the purchase of stocks by retail investors. I remember going to a shopping mall close to my home in downtown Toronto and being offered a credit card. I happily accepted it as a young man with no financial backing. Shortly after that, I met with one of my friends, who was a young musician. He also was happy that a credit card had popped up in his mailbox, so he could use that money to release his new album. At an Irish pub on a Saturday night, he told me with a big smile on his face that the bank didn't know how broke he was, otherwise they wouldn't have sent him the card, and then he laughed while drinking his beer.

This mania ended like any other one in the 2000 stock market crash when many dot-com companies defaulted on their financial obligations and went through mass liquidations. The crash wiped out half of the dot-com companies without a trace.

Soon after the burst of the dot-com bubble, there was a foreign attack on American soil for the first time in decades. The politicians decided to respond hastily to the terrorists in an equally powerful manner, so unfortunately instead of chasing and competing with the winners of globalization in East Asia, the decision was made to chase the losers of globalization in the remote mountains of Afghanistan, a country known to be the graveyard of old empires. These wars prolonged and resulted in further fiscal deterioration and indebtedness of the world economy. They also accelerated the decline of the global hegemon as well as the rise of an economic powerhouse in the East. This was analogous to the global conflicts of the last century, especially the 1930s and 1940s, when a rising power met with a declining incumbent empire.

Housing Bubble of 2008

Another bubble we can discuss together is the housing bubble of 2008. In order to understand this bubble, we have to understand the market participants in a bubble, including 1) the consumers or the citizens, 2) commercial banks, 3) investment banks, 4) credit rating agencies, 5) home builders and realtors, 6) international investors, 7) insurance companies, 8) governments and municipalities, 9) central banks and the governments, and 10) the market vigilantes. These entities created the housing bubble of 2008 as they acted according to their incentive base.

In the early 2000s, there was a genuine necessity for the continuation of exponential growth and compounding as the first requirement of a capitalist system, so the baton was passed from the tech industry to the housing sector. Let's not forget that a perpetual debt-based system needs constant expansion of debt to create more liquidity in an exponential fashion, so the housing market became the engine of growth for formation of new credit in the system.

The dominant notion was that houses always gain more value, and people considered buying houses as a great investment. Yes, real estate can be a great part of someone's portfolio, but when millions of people fully expose themselves to one asset, called housing, based on high leverage, it can certainly create either a hard landing or a very pernicious soft landing for decades to come; it can also cause a combination of both.

1) Consumers and Citizens

I personally remember house-flipping events that were packed with uber-enthusiastic people. During these courses, the lecturer would present a package from A to Z about how to profit from this abundant wealth called housing, and surely people loved it. These events were more like religious rituals or rock concerts than investment events, and the euphoric mania was felt everywhere. For the consumers, housing offered a great profit-making scheme. They could put as little as 5 or 10 per cent down and lever up ten or twenty times in order to magnify their profit-making machine. At some point in the bubble, NINJA mortgages were introduced, so somebody could get approved based on a low teaser rate with no income, no job, and no assets. Anybody who could fog a mirror or had a pulse was a potential candidate for purchasing a house. The consumers were convinced and incentivized that this was the way to prosperity.

2) Commercial Banks

The dominant notion for every commercial bank was that the loans were protected via their collateral, so any loan failure could be mitigated by foreclosing on the house. So they kept serving more and more liquor to the already drunken patrons until everybody got toxically drunk. They acted according to their incentives in order to generate more revenue in terms of compound interest payments collected on the mortgages. Commercial banks eventually had to sell loans to risky sub-prime clients with lower credit ratings, since they'd run out of prime clients, in order to exponentially grow the lending volumes required for continuation of the scheme.

3) Investment Banks

These banks also acted according to their incentives. Nobody wants to miss a bubble, especially if you can ride it to the top. It's even better if you're a good market timer, so you can short it on the way to the bottom. Investment banks gathered these mortgages, put them in separate baskets, got ratings on them, and sold them to international investors, pension funds, and mutual funds.

Due to the magic of investment banking, miracles happened. For example, Joe was a simple worker who'd lived in Alabama his entire life. He'd lived paycheque to paycheque most of his life, and he had a low credit history. He just bought a new house and got approved for a mortgage due to a low teaser rate that was set to expire in six months. Investment banking took Joe's mortgage, packaged it, and sold it as an investment product to international investors who sought safe dividend paying assets. In some instances, the investment banks shorted the same products that they sold to their own clients, knowing the poor quality of the packages.

Mortgage-backed securities, collateralized loan obligations, and collateralized debt obligations were amongst the hottest investment products of their time, so investment banks acted according to their role within the framework of law.

4) Credit Rating Agencies

Credit rating agencies also acted according to their incentives, since they're in a competitive business. They knew that their clients, investment banks, can leave and go to their competitors if they don't rate the packages favourably and generously.

5) Home Builders and Realtors

These entities also acted according to their own incentives. They tried to build and sell more and more houses in order to gain revenue.

6) International Investors

International investors also acted for their own profit, knowing that these financial products, later called the financial weapons of mass destruction, were highly rated and fully insured.

7) Insurance Companies

Insurance companies also insured these derivative products, knowing that they were rated as high-quality financial products by the agencies, so the insurance companies could also raise their revenue by expanding their horizons and selling new and profitable insurance packages that didn't exist before. They also knew that they were too big to fail, and they would be bailed out by the government in case of a black swan event.

8) Governments and Municipalities

Governments and municipalities loved the rise in housing prices, since it offered them more tax revenue via more buildings, more property taxes, and more activity in the economy. It also created a wealth effect that resulted in more spending and more tax revenue.

9) Central Banks and Market Watchers

Central banks also decided to let the free market reach the equilibrium on its own, since the accepted notion was that by pricking a bubble, you do nothing short of stalling the economic growth.

10) The Market Vigilantes

I have experienced a few bubbles in my life, and I realize that it's extremely hard and almost impossible to preach a view contrary to the dominant notion of the bubble, so the economists who tried to raise awareness were often pushed to the side as "doomers" and negative people who ended up with no audience.

It's contrary to human instincts and the incentive structure to reject a bubble.

The Chinese Housing Bubble

After the global financial crisis of 2008, the housing crisis spread its contagion all around the world. It affected the labour participation rates, commodity prices, and global trade everywhere. Some countries also ended up with sovereign defaults and austerity measures imposed on their economies.

Times were tough; however, the general notion in the world focused on unity and the fact that global collaboration would be maintained. Protectionism and beggar-thy-neighbour policies were generally rejected and despised. The notion amongst the elite was that we had learned our lessons from the Great Depression of the 1930s and were equipped with the so-called Keynesian Arsenal in order to fully remedy the crisis.

In the immediate aftermath of global financial crisis, it was believed that our global economy didn't need a reset, reform, or drastic makeover; instead, we could continue by just implementing a few patch-ups via monetary innovations and fiscal stimuli. The overconfidence of that era continued for a decade or two until it faded into a humble acceptance of the fact that this time was not different. A great part of that overconfidence came from the belief that miracles can happen in a fiat monetary system that is not based on gold; it was forgotten that exponential forces of compound interest always act the same way throughout time. It is true that in a fiat monetary system, the economy isn't held hostage to the discovery of new sources of gold, but a fiat system also suffers from boom-and-bust cycles of compound interest, which is the strongest force in the entire universe.

In 2008, Chinese elite also thought that their best plan was to use their fiscal and monetary capacity to provide the global economy with the liquidity that was absent. They believed that the rest of the world, especially the West, would get back on their feet soon, and China would pass the torch back to their Western counterparts. This would kickstart the global economy, and the Chinese would again export to the Western markets and buy the Western governments' bonds, so the globalization trend would continue normally after this blip. Furthermore, in 2008, the emerging economies, including China, carried much less debt compared to today, so the decision was made that China could rescue the world. Of course, it's easy to evaluate the outcome today and judge it, but at the time, it was a logical proposition.

So the Chinese started a multifaceted stimulus program that created a huge amount of displaced liquidity in their real estate sector. China made everything bigger compared to the rest of the world, including their ports, bridges, railways, and their ghost towns.

Until recently, the Chinese elite had one thing in mind—boosting their GDP by any means, even by building massive ghost towns and empty cities. They managed to build cities full of amenities, museums, and beautiful statues, with only one missing element: human dwellers. It's estimated that China has around 50 million empty houses that are used as investment vehicles. The price of houses has also increased in dramatic terms in the last couple of decades.

Many housing purchases have taken place due to speculation. A great proportion of sales were by citizens who already owned a house and were buying their second or third houses for speculative purposes. They even brought their speculative mood to Vancouver via the Chinese capital flight. I vividly remember those good ole times when foreign investment created a great boost to the Vancouver real estate market, but there was one problem: Vancouver became a city full of empty condominium buildings, to the point that the city dwellers had to leave the town and move to more affordable surrounding towns. It was simple—apartments turned into a speculative vehicle rather than a place to live in. The same phenomenon could be observed in Australia when Chinese investors placed multiple bids on every desirable house in Sydney and raised the prices to unreasonable levels.

In China, municipalities and the local governments used the housing bubble to their benefit to raise revenue for their expenses. Chinese municipalities bought the rural land cheaply, re-zoned the land, and then sold it as urban land to the developers at a much higher price. These types of land sales could account for 40 per cent of the local governments' annual revenue. Some construction companies in China grew in double digits for years and even decades, only to face a harsh collapse in recent times.

Like any other bubble, the forces of gravity appeared and put an abrupt end to the party during the early 2020s. These construction companies, and the financial institutions that had lent to them over the years, had to reinvent themselves. The financial institutions needed to reduce their lending exposure to the single and risky housing market and increase productive loans to the public. The Achilles' heel of every capitalist system is that as the system matures, there are always a few financial entities that have gotten fat and happy via lending to the housing sector over the years. When the housing bubble reaches its peak, these financial institutions have to remodel and reinvent themselves in order to abandon the non-productive mortgages; however, these obsolete institutions are usually unable to modify themselves, so they continue their old practices of mortgage lending and building new houses into the abyss. These financial institutions should find ways to generate productive loans to entrepreneurs and businesses that create real jobs in the economy rather than giving out mortgages to speculators who engage in bidding wars over scarce houses in desirable neighbourhoods in the big cities.

Another major issue with housing bubbles is that as the housing prices go up, citizens have to dedicate a greater portion of their income into servicing the larger and larger mortgages or rents. This creates less disposable income that can be spent in the general economy. As citizens dedicate more resources to service their housing, other sectors of the economy, including mom and pop shops, perish.

Higher housing prices also increase the cost of labour in general. The higher the rent, the higher wages should go up to pay for the shelter of the workers. This doesn't invite foreign investments into local productive industries like manufacturing and technology. This ignorance always results in the promotion of a bigger housing bubble, its consequential burst, and a systemic shock.

The Chinese are a little luckier compared to Japan and Europe, since their cycle hasn't yet matured as have many older economies, but they are about to face the harsh reality that the housing market can't grow in double digits for long before absorbing the severe side effects of an economic slowdown. Bursting the Chinese housing bubble could have a major, dangerous impact on the global economy, and it could also contribute to future Chinese decoupling.

In the case of further decoupling, the new agenda can be that China will produce and also consume rather than the old export-driven model to the West. This will bring a huge structural change to the world economy, considering the magnitude of China's exports to the West. The danger exists that in ten years, the world might become bifurcated into two separate Eastern and Western blocks that don't collaborate economically, socially, and politically due to protectionist policies.

It can be assumed that consumerism and consumption habits take time to manifest themselves in China, and it's premature to fully rely on Chinese consumers to entirely absorb the magnificent Chinese productive output yet, so it will take years for China to completely decouple from the West, if it happens. The Chinese have invested in bilateral trades using Renminbi or Chinese Yuan with many of their economic partners and have built some pipelines around the core global financial system, but they still lack the freely floating currency, global bond markets, global stock markets, and the derivative markets.

It can be presumed that the Chinese deliberately opted out of overgrowing their financial sector to prevent catching Dutch disease. Basically, having a valuable currency equals having a less productive manufacturing sector due to expensive exports. Chinese leaders are engineers, so they don't like to sacrifice their manufacturing base in order to build a large financial sector. A society run by engineers is different from a society run by lawyers, so China might never financialize its economy in a Westernized manner. Sometimes following textbook economic recipes can lead to losing your productive capacity as well as your relative technological advancements; having a somehow invaluable currency can be a blessing, since it can boost your manufacturing exports, which are the engine of creativity in any society. Your productivity is the main factor that enables you to reach your desirable potential, not your consumption.

China will go through lots of boom-and-bust cycles and also depressions with a capital D; despite that, it seems that China is on the rise to be in the driver's seat when it comes to global leadership. This is quite significant, since it will be the first time in many decades that the world faces this scenario, in which a rising power challenges the existing hegemon. It brings new societal, cultural, and economic norms that the world has never seen before. Having said that, we have a set of possible futures in front of us, not one certain future, so it remains to be seen how the future will evolve into reality when global superpowers interact and shape the new world order. My hope is that we never face a direct military conflict between the economic giants of the world. This will be the worst-case scenario and should be prevented at all costs.

China is also dealing with an ischemic population growth as well as an upcoming demographic decline, which will bring huge challenges to the supply of our global workforce. The only hope for solving this major issue is to fully integrate Africa and India into our global economy to compensate for it.

Another major factor affecting the Chinese economy is water. China needs to utilize its ingenious engineering capacity to overcome this threat, otherwise it won't survive as a great civilization.

I would like to add a personal touch to this section. I travelled to China as a teenager in 1993. I always remember the after-work rush hour in Beijing; it was overwhelming and amazing to see tens of thousands of Chinese workers going back home on their bicycles. They also seemed happy and had smiles on their faces. I am aware that those bicycle riders are driving cars now.

I also recently studied Mandarin for a few years. Although I miserably failed at it, the same way that I've failed at speaking English without a foreign accent, I had a chance to talk to average Chinese citizens who lived in Xi'An and Wuhan, and I learned about their concerns and aspirations. I learned that they are blessed with an ancient culture, traditions, and their own righteous social conduct. They are smart and hardworking people with a bright future. Their concerns were mainly the lack of political representation for the citizens, social injustice, social inequality, strict surveillance measures, a weak judicial system, and environmental pollution.

Although many structural changes need to take place in China and the rest of the world, I hope that the notion of global collaboration will return. It is the best option for all.

Cryptocurrency Bubble

This recent bubble is very similar to tulip mania of the seventeenth century. Crypto investment turned into a religion for many market participants. Crypto hysteria was everywhere. This time was different, since crypto was going to create a totally decentralized world and bring peace and prosperity to millions of people. You could hear about cryptos at every party and social gathering. My cousin, who lives in another country, used to call me often to inform me about this new miracle. She unfortunately sold her house in order to fully invest in crypto.

Some people thought of cryptocurrency as money, despite its huge volatility. Some people thought of it as a perfect speculative vehicle. Some people wrongly thought that cryptocurrency offered privacy in transactions. Some used it for sending money overseas. Some compared cryptocurrency to precious metals as the store of value. For some, it was their fanatic ideology and religion. Some other people righteously loved the block chain technology and its wonderful capabilities. I looked at cryptocurrency from a social perspective. I was well aware that its main promoters were young men, and I also knew that at later stages of capitalism, a significant number of young men become the so-called disenfranchised youth. Crypto was the perfect speculative tool for masses who don't want to leave their homes and want to live most of their time in the comfort of their room, with their laptops in their laps and playing video games, adopting a sedentary lifestyle.

In 2021, cryptocurrency hysteria reached its peak, which was the reminiscent of the tulip mania. You could even buy a house if you happened to have a few famous cryptocurrencies of the time. I remember talking to a younger millennial friend of mine during that time. He was strongly persuading me to buy cryptocurrency at the peak. He also suggested that he was ready for retirement due to his exposure to this sector of the market. We chatted for an hour, and I realized that cryptocurrency occupied 97.5 per cent of his portfolio, so I suggested that he needed to sell a portion of his cryptocurrency and use those funds to diversify into different sectors of the economy, or even to pay back his student loan. My advice to him was that cryptocurrency definitely had a place in everybody's portfolio, but it should be less than 5 per cent of the total assets.

He got very upset and told me that his particular crypto was going to reach $200,000 per coin very soon. His main argument was that if he had played the markets in a balanced and diversified manner since the beginning, he would never have ended up with so much precious crypto in his hand. He was proud of taking excessive risk in the past, which had paid off. My counter argument was that winning a Russian roulette game once or twice doesn't mean that you can continue safely down that path. I also tried to explain the volatile nature of cryptocurrency to him, since these cycles had happened before, but our conversation got very heated, and finally he said, "Fine, enjoy staying poor." Then he left.

In less than one year, in 2022, cryptocurrency crashed to the bottom of the barrel. The cryptocurrency of choice for many people lost roughly 75 per cent of its value at the peak and is still going down on daily basis.

This year, I tried to contact my friend via text messaging a few times to go biking together, but I haven't heard back from him. Thankfully, his social media page suggests that he's doing well, considering the fact that everyone presents a glorified version of their life on their social media page. I also talked to my aunt a few months ago. She told me that my cousin is doing relatively well, despite losing her entire house over her crypto investments. My aunt also told me a few stories that were indicative of my cousin somehow losing her mental stability recently. She has a very supportive family and soon will recover.

The Everything Bubble

After the great financial crisis of 2008, the risks mainly laid on the side of secular stagnation as well as deflation, the new mediocre, globally-synchronized distress, and the new normal. There were a lot of deflationary tectonic forces at play that needed to be mitigated with pro-inflationary financial innovations of the central banks and their associated governments all around the world.

The large amount of existing corporate, fiscal, and household debt was considered a deflationary force, since many entities were in balance sheet recession, and the cost of servicing their debt on monthly basis was a burden on the economy. It consequently reduced the velocity of money in the world. Some consumers spent less when they realized that they were in negative equity. Moreover, households ended up with less disposable income due to the rise of their monthly housing costs, which exhausted a greater portion of their salary on day-to-day basis.

After a bubble bursts, fearful people actively try to increase their principal payments rather than just the interest payment on their loans and mortgages, which brings a tighter squeeze on the economy. Social inequality also creates a wealthy minority that can't compensate for the lack of consumption by the indebted middle class. In addition, globalization is a deflationary force, since it reduces the price of labour, goods, and services around the world.

After the markets reach their bottom, typically consumers lose their willingness to borrow, and banks also become more cautious and raise their criteria for offering new loans to eligible candidates only. Trust becomes scarce when trust is needed the most, so banks don't even lend to each other, since they have doubts about the counter-party liabilities. Therefore, both central banks and governments have to come up with stimulus plans to compensate for the slack in the private sector. This way, they can hope to prevent a deflationary spiral.

It's a known fact that the most painful episode in a capitalist cycle is its deflationary spiral, so after 2008, there was a great determination to increase the money supply in order to battle deflation or even disinflation. The mission was clear, and the fiat monetary system also provided the governments with plenty of room to create liquidity, as shown here.

1) It started with TARP (Troubled Asset Relief Program) and continued with LSAP (Large Scale Asset Purchases) or quantitative easing to inject liquidity into the economy by purchasing financial assets that belonged to distressed entities. Later on, it was discovered that quantitative

easing might have had a reverse effect on the markets, since it removed the pristine collateral out of the repo market and created hardship for collateralized loans' initiation and rehypothecation.

2) ZIRP (Zero Interest Rate Policy) was tried.
3) ZIRP turned into NIRP (Negative Interest Rate Policy) in some European countries as well as Japan. To this day, a large portion of sovereign bonds hold negative nominal return due to this policy. It also had a detrimental effect on insurance companies, mutual funds, and pensions that rely on a real positive return in order to serve their clients. It's believed that NERP can work under severely deflationary circumstances and within limited utilization, but not in a disinflationary environment.
4) Operation twist was tried to modify long-term interest rates.
5) Forward guidance was also tried to guide markets into more optimism and exuberance.
6) Some countries tried yield curve controls in order to target the spread between different maturities.
7) Universal basic income, or helicopter money, was also introduced to many countries under different names in order to inject liquidity directly into the economy through millions of consumers.
8) Fiscal stimuli were tried in almost all countries around the world in different proportions and magnitudes, depending on the size of their economy. Fiscal stimuli came in the shape of bank bailouts, corporate handouts, federal loan forgiveness, universal basic income, and other government programs.
9) Debt restructuring has occurred in some regions of the world by softening the bankruptcy laws and availability of credit to entities after they claim for bankruptcy.
10) Last but not least, Brady bonds, or even perpetual bonds with no maturity date, were suggested as a tool in the toolbox.

These pro-inflationary measures could be considered drastic and unprecedented.

It can be said that the last couple of decades were the era of massive monetary innovation all around the world.

After fifteen years of optimism and trying to use every possible tool in the tool kit to reflate the global economy, this bubble, like all bubbles in history, burst in 2023 via an abrupt and furious rise in interest rates, which simply left the highly-levered market players in shock and awe. Like any other time in history, free markets prevailed and demanded a higher level of interest rate, which is the price of time. As I write this book, I can't fully comprehend or estimate the level of pain brought on by the bursting of the everything bubble, but my anecdotal observation suggests that it is yet to be understood.

Having said that, the inflationary and deflationary forces are like tectonic plates that are constantly in motion. Yes, lots of financial stimuli were provided to stimulate the economy, but we also had austerity, budget cuts, and a lack of organic formation of new loans by the private sector. Moreover, when central banks and governments create liquidity, it goes to different sectors of the economy at different times with different velocity, so some sectors might be in deflation and others might experience a boom at the same time. For example, fiscal stimuli can create a boom in stock markets and cryptocurrency, but it might not raise the standard of life for a farmer living in Alberta, Canada. Nobody, not even the central banks, can control the flow and velocity of the newly created money.

Some believe that all that financial stimuli provided by the governments and central banks created the everything bubble and resulted in the stragflationary environment, we're experiencing in 2023. Others believe that they didn't do enough to stimulate the economy to compensate for the private sector's slack. It can be claimed that the stagflation is the result of higher exogenous consumption that is taking place in the emerging markets, demographic issues that have tightened the labour market, supply chain disruptions, protectionism, and deglobalization. Therefore, it has nothing to do with the financial innovations of the last couple of decades.

The wiser notion suggests that our financial system is a complex system, and its complexity rises in an exponential fashion as it matures. Economic maturity expresses itself in the formation of systemic and core issues that can't be addressed with monetary policies. The system acquires structural and core deficiencies over time that can't be effectively resolved by monetary stimuli or financial innovations.

These are some of the systemic issues in the global economy that need to be addressed by the corporations, international institutions, governments, and citizens of the world:

- prolonged and large-scale global trade imbalances
- significant social inequality amongst citizens
- financialization of the developed economies
- de-industrialization of the developed economies
- a gargantuan derivative market that's like a giant asteroid that might hit the earth one day
- global debt saturation
- contingent liability of too big to fails that might fall of the edge of the table
- low velocity of money
- asset bubbles
- aging of the world population
- low birth rates in developed economies
- demographic cliff
- rise of useless consumers
- rise of disenfranchised youths
- lack of democratic rights in developing countries
- dictatorships in the emerging market regions
- lack of effective global governance
- multipolarity and global anarchy
- poverty in the developing markets
- weakening of the family unit
- fatherlessness
- hyper-individualism
- loneliness
- public health crises
- inequality of health outcomes

- global food shortages
- aging farmers
- reduction of organic farming
- malnourishment of populations around the world
- rise of public anxiety
- refugee crisis
- racism
- sexism
- decline in morality and ethics
- pension ponzi
- lack of fiscal sustainability
- rise of religious fanaticism
- rise of non-state political players
- rise of social diseases like alcoholism and drug abuse
- opioid crisis
- environmental pollution
- deforestation
- climate change
- global warming
- global pandemic
- rise of protectionism
- supply chain disruptions
- de-globalization
- global decoupling
- trade wars
- currency wars
- proxy wars
- unconventional weapons
- nuclear proliferation
- exhaustion of the Keynesian arsenal leads us to conclude as below.

The only hope is that the era of mass global awakening brings a new age of enlightenment to humanity via a united global consciousness, otherwise the bitter experiences of our great-grandparents in the 1940s will repeat in our lifetime. The global community needs to unite in order to deal with the enormous challenges ahead and prevent the mass extinction of humanity.

Global sympathy and collaboration are the best remedy left, and the global community can only hope that technology will also help to create a world that can overcome challenges and return to prosperity. Technology might bring us a productivity boom; in addition, empathy and sympathy will bring us global peace and collaboration that is desperately needed for our survival.

This new level of global sympathy and empathy should reach beyond race, culture, class, gender, and age for humanity to thrive.

I am an optimist.

Chapter Three

The Strongest Force in the Universe

In order to understand human biology, we need to understand a human cell. In order to fully comprehend capitalism and its cycles, one needs to fully comprehend compound growth and exponential functions, which is embedded in the core and essence of the system.

On a daily basis, we hear that the population of our city is going to increase by 10 per cent per annum. The GDP of a country grew by 12 per cent per annum over the last decade. The rate of inflation is 7 per cent per annum. The compound rate on your mortgage is 5 per cent per annum. What does it mean? Do we grasp the exponential mathematical functions in our daily lives? The human mind is an evolutionary byproduct and inherently observes the world in a linear fashion, so the answer is no, we do not grasp the exponential functions around us.

A 7 per cent inflation rate means that the person is going to lose half of his or her wealth and purchasing power in ten years.

Seven per cent inflation per annum means that in sixty years, which is lower than the average life expectancy of a person, a $2.50 coffee will cost $160.

Ten per cent population growth means that you need to double the size of your city, its amenities, and its social services in seven years.

A $1,000 payday loan amazingly carries an average interest rate of 400 per cent per annum and will cost the borrower $10 billion in only ten years.

If a country grows at double digits of 12 per cent per annum, you could expect the continuation of that trajectory will triple the size of that economy, triple the size of its debt, and even triple the size of its consumption in only ten years.

Compound growth is the best friend of an emerging economy. It creates a rapid rise out of poverty for the masses. The same force becomes our worst enemy when the economy matures and consequently faces limited environmental, demographical, technological, and natural resources required to support the continuation of compound growth. Exponential functions have been with us in our best and worst times in history during the boom-and-bust events.

Compounding laws also govern a country's monetary supply, and its aggregate debt that can result is disastrous hyper-inflationary outcomes as well as deflationary spirals. The exponential functions of compound interest always follow the same mathematical pattern and have created hyperinflationary events in history. The hyperinflation of the Weimar Republic was so devastating that people used to throw their cash into ovens just to warm their houses. There's a story that a German retiree took his life's savings during the hyperinflation of 1923 and could only buy one loaf of bread with it. This contributed to massive suffering in the German population that ended in them voting for an evil strongman who blamed the others for the misfortunes of Germany. History has shown us that the masses can resort to division and despair when economic cycles hit their downturn. This is also why, today, the German elite are one of the most conservative authorities when it comes to printing money, because they are well aware that they can't afford to forget the past.

I believe that we live in an era analogous to the 1930s, and we simply can't refer to our recent life experiences to grasp the reality of today's world. We need to review the dark historical events in order to prevent them from happening again.

Can hyperinflation happen again? Can it create a new monster again? Yes, if we're not aware, so we better learn to prevent it. Hyperinflation is a natural result of exponential functions and compound growth of money supply.

In the early twentieth century, Germany was the rising power that challenged the existing hegemony of the British Empire. Both countries had a lot of bilateral trade and common interests, but that didn't prevent the wars from happening.

In the early twenty-first century, China is the rising power that is challenging the hegemony of America. Although there's a lot of trade between these two countries, we are moving toward distancing and decoupling. The economies also are becoming mature, which means that we are getting closer to potential hockey-stick phase of compounding, which is the phase when growth shows its non-linear character and creates consequential conflicts that need to be prevented at all costs.

World War II cost humanity 80 million innocent lives, and at that time capitalism was only partially spread into a few continents. We cannot, should not, and will not allow a similar outcome, especially when capitalism is now global. A major conflict will affect 8 billion people all over the earth. Moreover, the existence of unconventional weapons like bio-weapons, tectonic weapons, nuclear armamentarium, and cyber arsenal makes any potential conflict ten times worse than what was experienced during the First and Second World Wars. Awareness is preventive.

In more recent times, laws of exponential functions created other hyperinflationary events in Argentina, Lebanon, Venezuela, and Zimbabwe. In Zimbabwe, the government created a $100 trillion note. I bought one of those notes as a joke, and later on it turned out to be a good investment, since the bill gained in value. I have a great friend from Sub-Saharan Africa who lives in Calgary, Alberta. He first-handedly experienced the hyperinflation over there, so he has been a great teacher and helped me understand how hyperinflation felt in Zimbabwe. We also came to the conclusion that no country is totally immune to hyperinflation, not even rich countries.

At the time of this writing, many regions of the world are experiencing stagflation, which can lead into an acute hyperinflationary event, a deflationary spiral, or a combination of both that can vary in different regions of the world, depending on how the mathematics behind compound growth will determine the fate of those societies. Let's engage in an imaginary experience to further understand exponential functions.

Imagine you are standing at the bottom of an empty Olympic-size swimming pool and are also tied to the ground. We try to fill this pool with only one drop of water; however, this drop of water doubles every minute, so it's fair to say that after the first minute, the swimming pool contains only two drops of water. These will be literally invisible in the pool. After the second minute, we end up with only four drops of water, which are also invisible, and so on. You might think that it will take centuries to fill a swimming pool this way. No, it only takes fifty minutes for the swimming pool to get filled by using one drop of water that follows the exponential functions of compounding. After forty-five minutes, the water only reaches your ankles, so you feel no threat to your life. It's only during the last five minutes of the experience that the pool gets completely filled up.

This is the natural indication of compound growth; it's not threatening and starts with a benevolent and linear growth until it reaches its hockey-stick phase and becomes destructive. It's why in the late stages of capitalism cataclysmic events can happen unexpectedly. This force works very slowly at the beginning of the cycle and then suddenly grows at an exponential trajectory, which can result in sudden bankruptcies and defaults.

This phenomenon is solely responsible for the booms and busts of capitalism. It's also responsible for the cyclical nature of our economies around the world. This is why we have always had an economic recession once every five to eight years as well as a big one every eighty years. At some point the system reaches the hockey-stick phase and collapses on its own weight, only to reset itself after a chaotic revolution, collapse of a civilization, an era of endarkenment, or a bloody world war.

No monetary or financial innovation in a fiat monetary system, gold-based system, or any other system can harness the power of compounding and exponential functions. At best, you can only delay the inevitable.

No matter how much liquidity you inject into a debt-based system, it won't quench the thirst for more, and more liquidity is needed when the system reaches the hockey-stick phase. I once watched an economist talking about the public debt in his country. He claimed that every president in recent times had doubled the public debt. I didn't have time to verify it, but I understood that such a situation is possible when the government creates money as debt, and the government services the debt by paying the interest only. Then you can end up with larger and larger additional increments of debt each year, to the point of doubling the debt every four to eight years.

At some point when the cycle matures, the private sector is no longer capable of absorbing the required acquisition of debt in order to create enough liquidity for the older debt to be serviced. Then central banks and governments try to fill that gap, not taking into consideration that they're fighting the most powerful force in the universe.

I believe that there's a deliberate act on the part of economists in general to make the economic arguments appear more scientific and even more complex. However, this one concept of exponential functions can explain years and years of economic jargon in a nutshell.

There is also a naive sense of optimism that the academic elite can control this force called "the eighth wonder of the world." The only way to deal with exponential functions correctly is to allow shorter and smaller five-to-eight-year cycles rise and fall without any interference by the monetary authorities, so that the larger eighty-year cycles won't overgrow to become a destructive force globally.

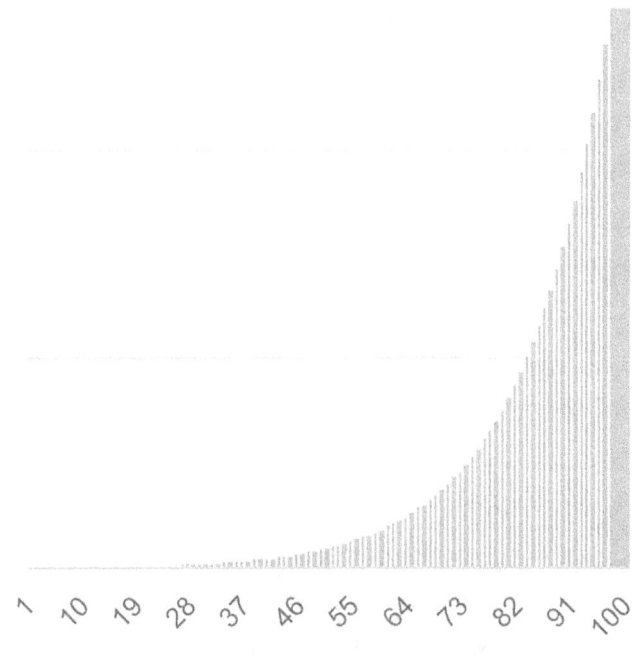

Compound growth at 7% per year over hundred years

Any attempt to smoothen the five-to-eight-year cycles by reducing the interest rates, asset purchases, or fiscal stimuli will result in an accumulation of these forces that will hit back with much higher velocity and destructive power at a later date in the long-term cycle. Some ancient cultures offered a seven-year jubilee in order to deal with the cycles. Our bankruptcy laws are to some degree inspired by it also. However, it's extremely hard to implement a debt jubilee every seven years while one's debt is considered somebody else's asset and placed in a daisy chain of derivative market bets.

It's beneficial to understand exponential functions by delving into a few simple mathematical equations that further help us mentally grasp compound equations.

Exponential function describes the size of any entity that grows steadily when the time for the growing quantity to increase by a fixed fraction is constant. Moreover, each added fraction is larger than any previous one in a sequential manner. Let's start with the simplest rule of exponential function, called the rule of 72. This rule was developed by Luca Pacioli in 1494. You have to take it with a grain of salt, since it can't be applied to all occasions, but it helps simplify more complex compound growth equations for day-to-day utilization.

The rule of 72 offers a simple way to calculate the doubling time of an entity that follows exponential functions:

$$T_2 = 72 \, / \text{ per cent growth per unit of time}$$

For example, if an economy grows by only 2 per cent per year, which is the number that is arbitrarily chosen for the developed economies as a target, you can expect that economy to double in thirty-six years, which is astonishing. The desired rate of 2 per cent per annum growth means that an economy of 300 million people will be an economy with 600 million population in thirty-six years if we keep the rate of consumption per capita, productivity, and debt per capita intact. It's feasible to double the size of a small economy in thirty-six years, but it's almost insane to double the size of a large economy in that time in real terms.

What about if an economy grows at 6 per cent per annum? If that economy serves a population of one billion people, we divide seventy-two by six, which results in a doubling time of twelve years. This economy needs to host two billion people in only twelve years without changing the productivity rate per capita. Is it even conceivable?

One of the major challenges with cycles of capitalism is that the population also grows due to the compound growth formula and exponential mathematics; governments encourage their citizens to procreate and increase the population, only to realize that the compound growth of population is severely out of line with the limited underlying physical resources, which can lead to mass human suffering during down cycles of capitalism.

Let's continue with a more accurate equation regarding compound growth. This formula is the foundation of our global economic system called capitalism:

$$A = P(1 + r/n)^{tn}$$

A: The Final Amount
P: The Initial Quantity
r: Compound Rate
n: The Interval
t: Time

Let's imagine that you invest $1,000 based on a 5 per cent interest rate that compounds annually for seven years. Let's calculate the final amount, not considering the underlying inflation rate.

P: the initial amount is $1,000
r: the compound rate is 5 per cent, or 0.05
n: the interval is on annual basis, which is one year, or 1
t: time is 7 years.

$$A = \$1{,}000\,(1 + 0.05/1)^{7 \times 1}$$

$$A = \$1{,}000\,(1.05)^{7}$$

$$A = \$1{,}407.10$$

The compound interest is a force that can turn $1,000 into $1,407.10 in seven years based on a rate of 5 per cent.

Let's imagine if we continue the same scheme for fourteen years. What would be the number using the above formula? It would be $1,979.93.

What about the total value of the investment in thirty years? That would be $4,321.94.

What if we continue our investment for seventy-five years, which is the average lifespan of an individual? Then we'll have $38,832.69.

A one-hundred-year investment will bring $131,521.26.

Exponential functions start in a desirable and linear fashion and end with a very curvy hockey-stick phase. The power of compounding over time manifests itself as the greatest force in the universe.

This equation is the foundation of capitalism that has reached every continent, every country, and every person in the twenty-first century. The fate of every citizen crucially depends on this single mathematical equation. The social inequality inherent in the late stages of capitalism is also the result of this mathematical equation. The earners of compound interest form the minority rich, and the payers of compound interest form the majority poor.

History is full of stories about how these two groups of people have interacted with one another through various events, including wars, revolutions, protests, riots, unions, elections, and social uprisings. This extremely powerful force, called compound interest, also brings the most dramatic problem with capitalism—the class divide. It matters to a great extent if the power of compounding is working for you or against you. This notion will one day end our global capitalist system.

Let's not forget that if a system is accepted at the moment all around the world, that doesn't guarantee its survival in the long run. For example, slavery was the accepted norm once. It established a widespread business model in many regions of the world during the colonial era. Slavery, the drug trade, and the arms trade were the dominant business models of the colonial era for the European traders who sailed to the newly found continents. Slavery was abolished as a shameful practice as humankind came to understand that the colour of your skin can't dictate your fate. Slavery is strongly and righteously condemned in the twenty-first century.

Feudalism was the dominant social model in medieval Europe. The nobility held the land, and the peasants gave the nobility homage, labour, and a share of the produce. Feudalism was also abolished when humanity grew out of it and realized that your bloodline cannot determine your wealth, power, and position in society. Anybody should be able to grow and reach the top echelons of society based on their talent, hard work, and merit. Humanity left feudalism for a more meritocratic system that rewards personal sacrifice, creativity, and the social contributions of each citizen.

Our relationship with capitalism is like the relationship of a fish with its fish bowl. If you've never experienced any other way of life, you don't understand what lies outside of this matrix, the same way that the fish doesn't recognize anything beyond that bowl; however, capitalism will be abandoned one day when humanity evolves, acquires more sympathy, and realizes that class cannot determine your fate and future in society, especially when the world's twenty-six richest billionaires own as much as almost four billion people on planet Earth. A top CEO of a company earns about four hundred times as much as an average employee. These figures show that despite the global reach of capitalism in the twenty-first century, its days are numbered in the long run.

I would like to share a personal story with you. I was honoured to serve the homeless population in Calgary, Alberta, for a couple of years regarding their dental needs. This experience changed my life, since it broke the stigma of homelessness in my mind. I realized that homeless people are truly wonderful human beings like you and me, but they have had a tougher set of cards to play with, and that's all. I used to eat lunch with them and listen to their stories. The place was full of conspiracy theories. I always knew that I shouldn't reject any story or suggestion, no matter how repugnant it got. I knew that ridicule and bias shouldn't have any place in my judgement, so I listened to all the stories.

One day, one of the friendliest members of the homeless shelter came to me and started telling me a story that shook me hard. He claimed that the elite who run our societies are not humans but reptilian extraterrestrials who have come here from another planet. He also showed me a few pictures of our societal elite; he suggested that their eyes are reptilian in nature, which proves they are reptiles under human skin.

That day, I was tempted to ridicule and dismiss his ideas by calling him insane, but I decided to never discredit anybody until they are scientifically proven wrong, so I continued thinking about his comments for a few days. I also thought about his personality. He had shown me a scar on his chest because somebody tried to stab his heart; he told me that he has been stabbed many times. He also had told me about not seeing his daughter for years due to his addiction and losing custody of her. He told me about stealing a car and bringing it to another province, but he never told me about his dad or about a loving relationship with his former spouse. He never told me about receiving love and care from his mom or his grandmother.

Suddenly, I had a eureka moment. I realized that the class divide in our society has become so wide that a homeless person who belongs to one extreme of this spectrum can no longer connect to the elite who occupy the other extreme. These two groups of people have totally different educations, upbringings, plans for their future, and lifestyles. They go to different places for vacation, if the homeless guy can afford a vacation. They have totally different plans for their children and different struggles and aspirations. They no longer connect as one entity. They have nothing in common.

Yes, they are extraterrestrials.

The class divide also hurts the so-called beneficiaries of capitalism, or the rich. Imagine being the 1 per cent of the 1 per cent and driving your latest Mercedes-Benz in your city with pride and joy. Your car offers you the best driving experience, with all the bells and whistles you desire. While driving and listening to your favourite song, you suddenly see a homeless person sitting on the curb and looking miserable. If you have even the slightest sense of sympathy in you, you realize that your whole day is ruined as you wonder: *How did she end up like that? Is she OK? Is she sick? Is she an IV drug user? What is she going to do in the cold? Why does she have a cup of blood beside her?*

You also can go to the most exotic places for vacation as the cream of the crop billionaire, but you still hear the daily news of people who live in poverty. My argument is that any person with a little sense of sympathy is not immune to the side effects of the severe social inequality in the world.

How do you feel about the mass shootings?

What about the victims of the pandemic regardless of how much wealth you have?

What is the boundary for one's suffering before you're affected by it emotionally?

Another inherent and core dilemma with capitalism is its incentive structure. Capitalism incentivizes every market player to create value in terms of dollars and cents; for example, a tree doesn't have any value in the system unless it's cut and sold as lumber in the markets.

Every economist refers to GDP as the most important measure to evaluate prosperity and functionality within the economy exactly the same way that a medical doctor refers to patient's vital signs in order to come up with a diagnosis; however, GDP is a very limited measure of prosperity at best; for instance, GDP does not value or count the loving contributions of a mother to her children including cooking, cleaning, hugging, and kissing them as a caring mom. GDP only starts to count her contributions when she offers her labour in the workforce.

Our annual GDP also measures our aggregate income in terms of sales value in one year, but GDP doesn't care about how it was achieved. For example, somebody might go to a college or have a wedding, and GDP goes up, or the same person might be murdered by being shot on the street; this also improves the GDP, since it increases the economic activity by engagement of the detective work, policing, and funeral services. These examples demonstrate that a system based on compound growth is inevitably subject to boom, gloom, and doom cycles, inequality, and eventual demise.

In the last example, we realized that a $1,000 investment can turn into approximately $131,000 based on an annual 5 per cent growth over one hundred years, considering nominal terms and not including the rate of inflation. What about debt? Do debt and expenses follow exponential functions? The answer is yes.

Let's calculate a total value of a mortgage, monthly payments, and the amount of interest paid by using a mathematical equation to represent it.

$$m = p.r / 1- (1+r)^{-n}$$

p: principle
r: interest rate
n: number of payments
m: the monthly payment

Let's imagine that the borrower acquired a mortgage for $300,000 with the fixed rate of 5 per cent over thirty years.

p: $ 300,000
r: 0.05
n: 30 X 12 = 360

$$m = 300,000 (0.05/12) / 1- (1+ 0.05/12)^{-360}$$
$$m = \$1610.46$$

The monthly payment is $1,610.46 before income tax. Now let's calculate the total payment for the mortgage over thirty years. We need to multiply the monthly payment by the number of months over the length of the mortgage.

Total loan cost = 360 X $1,610.46 = $ 579,765.60 (+ income tax)

Yes, it feels like you bought only one house for the price of two, which demonstrates the amazing power of compound interest.

Let's calculate the interest on the loan in order to understand why there's huge difference between the principal and the total cost of the loan over thirty years. We need to deduct the principal from the total cost of the loan.

r= 579,765.60 - 300000 = $279,765.60

I suggest that the expenses of a house also follow the exponential functions over thirty years of the loan term.

A $300,000 house can carry an annual property tax of $4,500 per year that grows at the rate of 7 per cent per annum. It also can carry a house insurance of $2,800 per annum that might compound at 7 per cent. The cost of repairs and maintenance can also add up to $5,000.

It can be estimated that it also grows at 7 per cent per year. The utility cost can be estimated around $2,000 per year and might grow at 7 per cent per year.

In order to calculate the total cost of a house over the term of the loan in thirty years, we need to calculate the above numbers using the exponential arithmetic. We also need to consider the cost of realtors, land transfer tax, mortgage insurance, lawyers' fees, and the capital gain taxes. These costs usually compound annually as well due to the underlying inflation.

The question arises as to why somebody even buys a house as an investment if it's so expensive to own one, and the answer lies in the fact that the growth of the price of a house also follows the exponential functions. For example, the value of a $300,000 house that grows at 7 per cent per annum is going to be estimated at $2,283,676.51 in the term of the loan, which is thirty years. You can also rent the house for an estimated $1,800 per month, which also might grow at exponential rates over thirty years. The result of your housing investment is only determined after these exponential entities that work both in and against your favour collide over time and present you with an outcome. Every investor is dealing with exponential functions, and their gain or loss is only determined by compound growth and exponential functions.

We also have to consider inflation as an exponential function that also can affect us in a negative way, unfortunately. Two notions should be understood in a differentiated manner in order to fully understand growth. We need to distinguish the real growth from the nominal growth. The real growth is only achieved after considering the underlying inflation or deflation in the market.

During inflation, your nominal growth exceeds real growth.

During deflation, your real growth exceeds nominal growth.

The etiology for inflation is the formation of new credit in the markets that changes the equation between supply and demand. In the majority of cases, inflation is a monetary phenomenon. However, inflation can also be a political phenomenon when countries implement protectionist policies and weaponize their exports to each other. Scarcity of goods and supplies can result in inflation without excessive rise in credit. Inflation reduces your purchasing power, while deflation is supposed to increase your buying power over time.

Imagine that your great auntie passes away and leaves you with $100,000 in inheritance. You're also a responsible person and decide to save it for your rainy day as well as the time that you get old and frail. Call it the retirement fund.

For the sake of simplicity, let's say that the price of each egg at the grocery store is roughly around $1, so your purchasing power at the moment is equal to 100,000 eggs. Imagine that you place your cash in a chequing account that pays no interest to you over time.

We want to calculate your purchasing power in thirty years at your retirement time with two different rates of inflation: 7 per cent per annum and 15 per cent per annum. Using the above formula, in thirty years under the 7 per cent inflation rate, you'll be able to buy only 13,000 eggs, so you'll lose 87,000 eggs up to your retirement time. In thirty years under the 15 per cent inflation rate, you'll be able to buy only 1,500 eggs and will lose 98,500 of your eggs up to your retirement time.

Who wants to break 98,500 eggs in their lifetime? How do you even clean that mess? This is a true example of dealing with exponential functions and their effects on everyday life.

That's why you put your eggs in different baskets, including housing, the bond market, the stock market, and even crypto to implement both inflationary and deflationary hedges in your portfolio, especially during times of unusual uncertainty.

Germans who had cash and lived during the hyperinflation of the Weimar Republic lost all their wealth; however, Germans who owned stocks in reliable companies, like Siemens, preserved their wealth through the turmoil of World War II and even beyond. Owning real estate in Germany at that time was a risky business depending on which side of Germany you ended up in; the real estate in West Germany appreciated, while Eastern Germany went to ruins under communism.

The power of compounding also can act in reverse. Deflation is a rare situation in which the economy experiences a shortage of liquidity due to the high burden of a large amount of existing debt, so the velocity of money as well as disposable incomes go down significantly. In this situation, negative interest rates are implemented, but you can still have a positive real return despite the negative nominal return; for example, if the economy shrinks at 3 per cent per annum, and you receive – 1 per cent nominal return on your savings account, you still have a positive spread of 2 per cent in real terms. It means that your real purchasing power is still increasing even with negative interest rates during deflationary times. I tend to believe that a deflationary spiral is the most adverse outcome that can be encountered, due to the lack of capacity to service debt under this condition. The Great Depression of the 1930s is a great example of a deflationary spiral.

All we wanted to achieve in this chapter with all this mathematical jargon was to show you that whether you like it or not, we live in the world of exponential functions, compound growth, and non-linear entities when it comes to our investments, population, government policies, and economic growth. In the world of exponential functions, there's a lot of room to gain as well as to lose, since everything is more powerful, exponential, and non-linear.

Chapter Four

Market Psychology

In order to understand market cycles, we need to understand the mathematical forces behind them, as reviewed in the last chapter; however, we can't appreciate the boom-and-bust cycles of the markets without exploring market psychology and the psychology of market participants. We need to understand humanity. We need to understand who we are in order to understand why capitalism has always been accompanied by severe boom-and-bust cycles.

A simple rule to understand is that cycles of capitalism are based on small, prolonged, and incremental gains over the long term, followed by abrupt and sudden, massive losses. It's the result of market psychology as well as boom-and-bust cycles of compound growth. These cycles can be called greed and fear cycles, and in order to understand reflexivity in the markets, we need to understand humanity.

Who are we? Humankind is an entity that is capable of showing tremendous sympathy when living in a civil society abiding by the rules of the nations, but at the same time, humans are subject to emotional decision-making based on herd mentality, fear, greed, and animal instincts, especially when it comes to financial markets.

Some market participants implement logic and high cognitive behaviour when participating in the markets; however, that's certainly not the case for the majority of investors.

Let's not forget that our primitive brain, or the emotional brain called the limbic system, is much older in evolutionary terms compared to our frontal lobe and the grey cortex in charge of reasoning. This is why I read a few books about chimpanzees in order to understand humans better. After all, we are family. I don't say it to degrade humans; I believe both chimpanzees and humans have good and bad traits that can be seen under the right conditions.

It's exactly the chimpanzee brain that creates a huge sell-off when fear of loss prevails over greed in the markets due to the herd mentality of the market participants. So when we talk about cycles of capitalism, we need to think about powers of compound growth that work hand-in-hand with emotional reflexivity of the market players. This further intensifies the boom-and-bust cycles of capitalism.

Now let's talk about kindness. Kindness is an inherent emotion in humanity that is embedded in every human being. I don't know how to even start describing the amount of kindness I've received from my fellow human beings, including teachers, friends, instructors, neighbours, classmates, colleagues, and so forth. I'll just put it this way. Once in my life, I witnessed a total stranger risking his life in order to rescue a drowning person in the Niagara Falls region. He took his clothes off and jumped into the river.

I've seen a picture of a young man who used his own body as a shield to protect his wife during the mass shooting in Las Vegas a few years ago.

I've heard the news that a mother and her baby who were trapped under earthquake rubble survived for a few days until rescued, since the mother fed her baby using her own blood.

I've heard about a doctor who passed away after working for seventy-two hours non-stop until he died helping his patients.

Twenty years ago, I had the pleasure of becoming friends with a World War II veteran. During one of our conversations, he mentioned that his life expectancy for his mission was estimated at eleven days, but he still continued as a pilot despite the horrible odds for survival.

We realize that kindness is an evolutionary trait embedded in every human being over millions of years of evolution, but the same is true about greed, especially when it comes to investing. The same inherent evolutionary trait is responsible for exaggerated cycles when the majority of market participants buy based on irrational greed and sell based on irrational fear of loss, without any logical justification.

Compulsivity also plays a huge role in market fluctuations, particularly among male participants. Some chase an asset price like our ancestor hunter gatherers chased a gazelle for hours and days for food. The hunter gatherer mind is still alive amongst modern human beings, and it's responsible for market volatility and abrupt fluctuations.

I've always been fascinated by nature, and I believe that although humans carry a lot of good emotions and instincts, including sympathy and kindness, we've also carried a lot of obsolete subconscious hunter gatherer traits into the modern world, and they are of limited use.

The combination of mathematical swings of compound growth and its interaction with the human psyche determines the fate of markets and capitalism in general.

Let's talk about a few emotional traits that modern society still manifests in order to prove that the hunter gatherer brain is still alive and in charge of the markets. Jealousy and promiscuity are considered evolutionary behaviours that still exist in our society. Jealous men had a higher chance of raising their own offspring, and those genes passed on to the next generations more effectively. Promiscuous women also had a better chance of raising healthy children by having access to a lager gene pool, and those traits also passed on to the next generations.

We also can understand why some people can't stop eating sugary food, since the evolutionary brain always conceived anything sweet in nature as safe and useful. Today, for the first time, sugar is abundant, and our evolutionary brain needs more time to design a stop lever mechanism for sugar through random mutations that need hundreds of thousands of years to happen.

Greed is still with us, since our ancestors who were greedy and hoarded resources had a higher chance of passing through a harsh winter without dying of cold and hunger, so those greedy genes survived and stayed in the human gene pool despite the fact that greed is no longer necessary in our modern society to survive.

Anger was needed for a hunter gatherer who hunted with primitive tools and needed a physical fight to kill a mammoth, but we still have that emotional trait when the stock price goes down. We feel the same primitive sense of loss and desperation.

Fear was needed for a hunter gatherer to run away from a predator, like a tiger, but that type of fear manifests itself in irrational market decisions. It's why people are fearful of declining stock prices, and that starts a selling frenzy. That is the herd running away from the predator.

People are fearful of spiders but not of collateral debt obligations. Our evolutionary mind has learned to be afraid of snakes and spiders over millions of years, but it has never dealt with mortgage-backed securities; however, the latter has negatively affected a lot more people in recent years. Markets crash due to evolutionary fears of the market participants rather than logical fears.

We have a grey cortex at our frontal lobe of the brain that has helped us think throughout generations; however, this part of the brain is not efficiently used by all members of society. I can argue that the limbic system as well as our emotional brain are in charge most of the time, even regarding our important decisions through life. This is called the subconscious mind.

Market psychology suffers from herd mentality as well as recency bias. It's natural for the subconscious mind to assume the current market condition is going to continue endlessly. At some point in the cycles, there is a rude awakening for the herd that the market conditions have shifted. This creates a mass flight to the exit door and tears down the whole financial system.

The psychology of calm and trust turns into fear, and market participants go to fight, flight, freeze, faint, follow, and fail mode. It's the time for irrational masses to sell off in the markets, which ends a prosperous financial cycle. These emotions of fear, greed, trust, lack of trust, envy, compulsivity, and stupidity are at play to form these up and down cycles at all time.

I had a friend who was a dealer at the casino. He told me that every night, he hosted desperate people in front of him who were throwing their retirement away on that gambling table. He said they looked desperate but still threw bags of money at him, and he didn't know why. I knew the answer; it was simple greed. This evolutionary trait is fuel for compulsive gambling and betting against the odds. The gambler is satisfying his or her true animal instincts. Capitalism appeals to your own greed rather than your virtues in order to create economic growth. The same can be said for lottery tickets, which are called the stupidity tax. Stupidity is also a strong force driving the markets.

The accumulation of debt in the late stages of capitalism also creates a sense of restlessness and fatigue amongst the majority of the population, and this increases their desperate attempts to get rich quick by unconsciously betting against the odds at casinos and lottery shops.

The evolutionary brain is a pleasure-seeking vessel, which is why the majority of investors seek pleasure by buying and selling stocks just for the dopamine surge rather than a purely logical approach to investment. If humankind was a solely logical entity, we'd all be Buddhist monks living in peace, but the human spirit can't enjoy itself just by sitting in a room.

If you look at humankind as the byproduct of random mutations over billions of years in an evolutionary process, it is sound to view other species to learn about humans, since we took the same journey before we diverted somewhere in the evolutionary chain. For example, it can be said that by analyzing a bacterium, you can learn about a human cell, since a human and a bacterium shared the same evolutionary pattern until they separated their journey at some point in evolution. In the case of bacteria, we shared the same evolutionary pattern, and we diverted about two billion years ago. In the case of chimpanzees, we share a common ancestor that lived around six million years ago, so that's why I sometimes study other species to learn about market psychology.

To understand more about the subconscious mind, we can argue that the colour green gives us calm and relaxation, since in nature it's the sign of fertility and accessible food, so our evolutionary brain is calm and relaxed when we go to a cottage out of town in the presence of water and vegetation.

Listening to crickets also makes you relax, since the evolutionary brain has heard that sound for millions of years. You can sleep like a baby listening to waves on the ocean, but you can't sleep at all if your house is close to a highway. The evolutionary brain isn't used to the sound of traffic, but it truly recognizes the ocean.

Shopping also has therapeutic effects for many people, since the evolutionary mind considers taking possession of stuff as a means of survival. In many cases, the market players and traders treat buying and selling stocks as shopping therapy rather than logical investment.

The evolutionary brain also doesn't have a stop mechanism when it comes to asking for dopamine rewards via trading on brokerage platforms, much the same way that video games affect the brain. Video game addiction is another modern phenomenon that affects the evolutionary brain. In nature, our hunter gatherer ancestors needed to accomplish a real task in order to receive a dopamine reward; however, our modern technology has created a box that gives the evolutionary brain intense and frequent dopamine surges, so it's no wonder we have this phenomenon called "video game addiction" amongst our youths these days. The same analogy applies to constant and continuous buying and selling of stocks via brokerage apps on smart phones by day traders.

Let me finish this chapter with a story about my dear Archie, who was a World War II veteran I had a pleasure to know in the early 2000s. I met Archie when he was eighty-three years old and used to sit on a bench in front of our apartment building to watch the birds. I also was a young, new migrant to Canada who wanted to talk to Canadians and learn about their culture. Luckily, Archie and I formed a meaningful friendship, talking to each other on a daily basis on that bench. Some of the stories he told me didn't make logical sense to me as a young man. For example, he told me that his life expectancy was estimated at eleven days during some of his missions, but he still continued on those missions, despite losing his best friends and comrades. When I asked why he'd risked his life to that extent, he never gave me a good answer. He just laughed and said, "What else should I have done?"

Once Archie told me that even horses that carried their equipment stopped after seeing the front men explode into pieces, but he still continued moving toward the front line, ignoring the potential dangers. Unfortunately, Archie and I never truly found out what made him risk his life to that extend. Eventually he was transferred to a seniors' house, and I never saw him again on that bench.

A couple of decades later when I was hiking in the beautiful Rocky Mountains of Alberta, I met a group of cute mountain gophers. I had plenty of time to observe their behaviour, since I was on my vacation. I observed that anytime a hawk got close to the colony, one of them stood on his feet and screamed in a very high-pitched voice to alert his friends. By doing this,

this cute gopher made himself more visible to the hawk and increased his chances of being caught as prey, but he still did this to save the lives of the others. Suddenly, I stood up and said, "Hi, Archie." I named that cute gopher Archie. It was the moment that I fully realized why Archie did what he did as a soldier. I gave all my peanuts to Archie and left with a satisfying answer that humans mainly act based on their instincts, which we share with other mammals, even when it comes to complex subjects like martyrdom and sacrificing yourself for your fellow humans.

Market psychology and evolutionary instincts are deep and important factors in creating up-and-down market cycles that have roots in the market players' subconscious minds. This force, which goes hand-in-hand with up and down cycles of exponential functions, can create dangerous and volatile swings that affect millions of people around the world.

One of the major flaws of today's economic textbooks is that they mainly view the science of economy as a purely mathematical entity. They totally dismiss the role of human emotions in the equation. The correct approach should be to understand that finance is a separate entity from economics, and it's a derivative of human reflexivity toward the underlying economy.

Chapter Five

Stages of Capitalism

If you ask me if I like capitalism, I'll answer with, "Which stage of capitalism do you mean? Capitalism can manifest itself in different shapes and forms, according to its maturity. A debt-based system manifests itself differently, and sometimes in an opposing fashion, due to the velocity and availability of capital or credit at each stage.

In this chapter, I'll explain how cycles of capitalism start, evolve, mature, and die off. These cycles have profound effects on attitude, health, wellbeing, and the behaviour of people who live through these cycles.

Let's divide capitalism into three cycles: 1) early-stage capitalism, 2) mid-stage capitalism, and 3) late-stage capitalism. This chapter will discuss the evolution of these cycles as they mature in time.

Early-stage capitalism usually starts after a major global or regional reset or reform due to the end of a big war, a global paradigm shift, or after a revolution. At this stage, there are two important factors: 1) there is little debt, and 2) there is little capacity. These two factors are beneficial to start compounding growth successfully. For example, Germany and Japan were losers of World War II, but they had a boom for a few decades after the war ended, as a new global financial reset helped them get rid of debt. They also had to build all their capacity and infrastructure that was destroyed in the war.

China in the 1990s experienced a paradigm shift from communism to capitalism, which enabled them to start compound growth for decades. Early-stage capitalism started in parts of China that were predominantly rural, which is another characteristic of the early-stage capitalism. Rural settings are fertile ground for cheap labour. They also offer a fertile ground for baby booms to come when the early stage kicks off. Another advantage of a rural setting is access to cheap organic food, which guarantees healthy and motivated workers for the constructions and creation of the infrastructure. Rural populations are more than motivated to change their humble circumstances and improve themselves to the middle class by working hard.

Luckily, I travelled to China during their early-stage cycle in the early 1990s, and I witnessed the exuberance in everybody's face. During the after-work rush hour, I witnessed tens of thousands of workers on bicycles going back home with huge optimism and joy. I could view the smile on their faces. They also didn't shy away from chatting with me, even with poor communication due to our different languages.

Early-stage capitalism is filled with joy. The majority of the population is leaving poverty and entering the middle-class level. There is lots of happiness and confidence that a new era has begun.

Early-stage capitalism in Canada can be described as the time in the late nineteenth century as well as the twentieth century after World War II. In Alberta, land reforms a century ago allowed people to migrate here and gain free land. They could use that land as collateral for loans, which created ample liquidity for the economy.

The gilded age was the true manifestation of the early-stage miracle of capitalism. In the United States, the rise of so-called robber barons in the late nineteenth century was due to jealousy toward the new billionaire class; however, it created a huge positive force to industrialize the nation into an industrial powerhouse.

The United States also had another early-stage capitalism after World War II, when there was a new financial reform called the Bretton Woods Agreement, followed by a baby boom and demographic strength. There is no doubt that there was an enormous sense of confidence and a can-do attitude in America post-WWII. One way is to listen to lyrics of the songs back then and sense the amount of joy, exuberance, and confidence in the music of that time. The song "My Way," released in 1969, is a good example of confidence, optimism, and a sense of pride in that era.

Early-stage capitalism is free of bureaucracy, as there's no need for complex structures of governance. The economy grows on its own due to its demographic strength, demand, and organic formation of credit.

In early-stage capitalism, the miracle is happening everywhere. People are getting out of poverty into an industrialized nation. It usually starts with the textile industry and is followed by toys, kitchen appliances, automobiles, and high-tech production. During early-stage capitalism, debt is a motivating factor that can be managed and paid off. The interest and principal are both payable by the borrower. Debt is not a burden on the society, since debt to GDP is very benign. With each new dollar of debt, GDP grows and multiplies organically.

During early-stage capitalism, production and productive jobs are abundant, which results in a small service sector and small government but a large industrial and farming sector. The leaders of the society are mainly industrial leaders.

Early-stage capitalism has very little to no taxation, since the government carries very little debt and very little promises to pay. Low taxation paves the way for a booming economy.

The competitive spirit is everywhere, and no entity has dominated the markets, which enables further innovation and progress amongst market players and corporations.

During early-stage capitalism, bringing children into this world is affordable, especially in a rural setting, so a baby boom follows and helps grow consumption and demand for the new products that are necessary for life. The medical field is also able to bring drastic and useful treatments to the public, like the invention of antibiotics and effective vaccines, which enhances life expectancy in the nation tremendously.

Families, communities, and societies are cohesive enough to solve their issues, so there is much less need for interventions by the lawyers, consultants, social workers, and police in the service sector. Society is more concerned with building the infrastructure, including roads and bridges, rather than suing one another. Social securities offered to the public are limited, since the workers are self sufficient and don't need to pay high taxes to the government. The workers aren't severely indebted, so they can save their capital for the rainy day without asking the government for help.

During early-stage capitalism, there is a sense of satisfaction at every level, so it's the norm for somebody to work in a company for a lifetime with absolute loyalty and then retire with enough wealth to sustain himself or herself.

As the economy matures, the infrastructures are built and a sense of confidence and a can-do attitude grows. Governments also offer more rights to their citizens, including pensions and free health care, since the government can afford to promise big. Political leaders are usually respected and charismatic, since a sense of prosperity prevails everywhere, and politicians make more and more influential and historical speeches to the public.

During the early-stage capitalism, there is a widespread sense of confidence amongst people, which represents itself in the elite of the society, including prominent scientists, directors, university professors, and industrial leaders. Well-known and respected agencies bring cutting-edge technologies to people in terms of space exploration, communication, and manufacturing.

This era represents the we-can-do attitude of the post-war economic environment in the United States. One American elderly man told me that anytime he travelled to Ohio and Lake Erie in the 1950s, his shoes and shirt got covered with dirt due to smog in the air, but he loved it. For him, it was the manifestation of American industrial might at that time.

Early-stage capitalism has one distinct feature, and that is the availability of capital amongst the market participants. Most people have assets with no collateral loan attached to them. This brings a lot of strength and prudence into the market. During early-stage capitalism, the investor has to invest with his or her own capital, so the investor uses more prudence and care compared to an investor who invests with borrowed money and credit. When you invest by using credit, you might as well say, "If somebody is crazy enough to lend me money, then I'm going to do stupid stuff with it." When the investor has skin in the game and places bets using his or her own capital, the investor does his or her due diligence, which reduces misallocation of resources to almost zero.

During this stage, there are no asset bubbles yet, so it enables young people to work hard and one day own a house without being indebted for the rest of their lives. Education also can be attained cheaply. I once talked to a health care professional who'd gone to dental school in Alberta in the 1960s. He told me that he could pay his tuition via a summer job at the local grocery store. These days, graduates carry more than half a million dollars in debt, which takes a lifetime to pay back. In early-stage capitalism, creation of debt creates a significant amount of income and GDP due to high velocity of money. The newly created money doesn't go out of circulation in order to pay the principal for the last debt, so the money multiplier works in favour of the middle-class.

Having said all of this, if you ask me if I like capitalism, I'll answer, "Yes, I love early-stage capitalism, during which the greatest power in the universe, compounding, is your friend." In this stage, compounding creates a boom when it comes to quality of life.

Social inequality is very mild or non-existent in this stage, which enables societies to have a united and family-like environment for all. Families are strong, and usually one parent's income is enough to support the whole family, which enables the other parent to emotionally, nutritionally, and lovingly support their children. Children are well supported and loved in families of early-stage capitalism in most instances.

Workers don't need to service a high level of debt and taxation, so the labour is cheap and profitable for the capitalist to hire, which results in a healthy job market. The relationship between the capitalists and the citizens is at best level since the citizens are able to both produce and consume as effective promoters of the system. Workers can also buy cheap housing, since the asset bubbles haven't arrived yet at this phase, so there's no need for servicing a large mortgage for the working class.

Early-stage capitalism might last for one or two decades in most cases, and then capitalism enters the mid-stage. Mid-stage capitalism is the stage when the maturity of the economy starts to show its effects on societies, and compound growth faces the challenges of limited underlying resources.

Mid-stage capitalism is accompanied by a great sense of confidence amongst people who have moved out of poverty and into the middle class.

For example, a person who used to ride a bicycle to work now has a middle-class small car. Most of the population is settled in urban areas and the cities rather than villages, but the important phenomenon that is often neglected is the concept of middle-income entrapment.

During mid-stage capitalism, people still believe that the ascent will continue without air pockets, ignoring the fact that rising from the middle class to the upper middle class is a whole new ball game. I can go even further and claim that the majority of the middle class are going to struggle to even maintain their lifestyle, let alone move to the upper middle class. For example, a taxi driver might now feel that he needs to put in more hours and drive in a more polluted environment to maintain his family's lifestyle.

During mid-stage capitalism, the rise of debt slows down the velocity of money in an insidious manner, but it's not realized as a major threat by the public. People, companies, and the governments can service their interest on the debt, and they can still borrow in capital markets without too much hassle. Some entities might realize that it's impossible for them to ever pay back their debt, including principal and the interest, but they can still maintain a positive equity and profitable portfolios, as long as the cash flow is there. Debt can be serviced, and new debt is organically created via bank loans in the private sector.

During middle-stage capitalism, the capitalists realize that it's no longer profitable to maintain their assembly lines and factories. Manufacturing becomes expensive, so outsourcing starts to form. Jobs always will be transported to countries in early-stage capitalism with cheap labour eager to join the middle class. Mid-stage capitalism is still industrialized, but it's in the phase of diverting itself from producing manufacturing goods. It manifests itself by a shift from manufacturing to the service economy, as labour is moving toward being more and more expensive. Labour now has to deal with the expenses of a middle-class lifestyle. The cost of servicing household debt has risen as well, and an urban lifestyle is more expensive than rural living and requires more expensive consumption.

There is also over-capacity. For example, people who sold their bicycles and bought cars soon realize that the roads are getting busy with new cars, and they have to deal with heavy traffic jams every day. Water isn't as clean as before, because the factory down the road has been polluting the lake for the past twenty years, and now it shows its harmful accumulative effect. There are already significant apartment buildings in the neighbourhood, which has taken a toll on the sewage system. During mid-stage capitalism, signs start to appear that there is an over- capacity, considering the limited resources. The environment also starts to show signs of duress; for example, more children might be diagnosed with asthma due to air pollution.

In mid-stage capitalism, the family unit is still strong, but both parents need to work in order to support the family, so children are left with paid strangers in order for parents to work and pay their expenses. Parents also become aware of these challenges and have fewer children, which will later manifest itself as a demographic cliff.

Farming also becomes more expensive, as does manufacturing, so imports of food rises. Corporations have to increasingly provide the population with cheap, processed food rather than organic and wholesome food. This will create a future health crisis and will compromise the labour force in the next few decades.

In mid-stage capitalism, powers of compounding are showing their true nature, and the exponential growth hits the limitations of growth due to political, environmental, and demographic limits and obstacles. Of course, the real economy can't grow in an exponential fashion for long, so the abstract economy keeps growing at the exponential rate, including real estate, finance, insurance, and the service economy.

Mid-stage capitalism comes with more private ownership of resources, which brings social inequality to the equation in a pernicious manner. A class society starts to take shape and form in this stage, but the class divide is not yet so disgustingly obvious. In mid-stage capitalism, people of different incomes can still go to the same restaurants and have the same hobbies by and large. The class divide can still be ignored at this level.

In mid-stage capitalism, the structural problems with the economy slowly begin to rise, including social inequality, financialization of the economy, trade imbalances, demographic slack, declining productivity, reduction in velocity of money, rise of debt to GDP, and lack of manufacturing. However, they go unnoticed, since every issue is at its early phase.

The GDP of the country also shifts from positive aspects of life to negative ones. As I mentioned before, GDP is neutral to the fact that income can be made by serving positive services to positive aspects of life, like education, travelling, manufacturing, and housing. The same GDP can be made by murder investigations, crimes, police services regarding shootings, sickness of people due to malnutrition, and medical services to chronically ill patients. In mid- stage capitalism, we start to view a shift from positive aspects of life to negative ones. For example, domestic assault might boost GDP by keeping lawyers, judges, and secretaries busy, but it's an income due to the decline of a society.

Mid-stage capitalism is also when very large corporations start to appear and form a less competitive environment by bankrupting mom and pop shops, which also reduces the availability of local jobs to the society; having said that, the spirit of competition still exists amongst the market players despite the initial rise of monopolies.

As the economy matures into late-stage capitalism, systemic problems start their visible manifestation. Trade imbalances signal worrying signs. The financial sector reaches its abnormal weight compared to the real economy through gargantuan derivative bets, and mega-corporations rise with contingent paper liabilities that fall off the edge of the table. Social inequality provides an acute contrast between rich and poor that is easily detectable by taking a simple walk in your downtown. The accumulation of debt, over-reliance on credit, and growth of debt to GDP visibly introduces a gloomy prospect.

During late-stage capitalism, lots of social engineering methods are introduced to the public with significantly unknown effects, and the effects aren't immediately felt due to the maintenance of consumption via credit. For example, you can severely suppress productive capacity in the society, but the effects of that can be postponed because you can use credit and maintain your consumption rate based on imports. You only feel the effects of outsourcing of jobs when it's too late and you have effectively fallen behind in the global technological and geopolitical competition. It might be too late when you find out that healthy productivity is needed in every society in order to create value, discipline, and defence via military means. In another instance, you can continue having a very low birth rate until it's too late and you encounter a demographic enigma.

During late stage capitalism, the economy moves toward creating abstract forms of wealth compared to real and tangible assets. The more the economy matures, the more paper wealth is created. A bigger share of the economy is dedicated to stocks, bonds, puts, options, and calls rather than producing eggs, bananas, and cellphones. Further progress in financialization of the economy results in totally abstract ideas like cryptocurrencies and NFTs, which shows that the finance sector has to climb the abstraction ladder even further into Alice in Wonderland stories in order to create value.

Lawyers and accountants deal with more abstract corporate structures away from the real and tangible world. The real risk arises when the magnitude of abstract wealth grows disproportionally to the real economy, to the point that the abstract assets become no longer redeemable in real terms. These events are horrendous, since markets stay quiet and ignorant about accumulation of abstract wealth for decades, until suddenly, global markets have a sudden and rude awakening that jacks up the interest rates to the moon, evaporating the whole economy in this process—like a forest fire that burns good and bad all together.

A simple comparison between the fields of medicine and finance can demonstrate how irrationally over-expanded the field of finance can become. All the medical doctors should be licensed in order to practice medicine, and some of these medical associations, universities, and colleges have been around for centuries in order to create a field for educating and organizing medical doctors. However, out of nowhere a hedge fund manager can have a lot more influence on society compared to a doctor, and the hedge fund manager has no licensing requirements. He or she can start their career with much less preparation compared to a physician. Furthermore, they deal with less regulation and supervision of their day-to-day performance. The infrastructure to attract talented people, educate them, and govern them throughout their finance career is simply lacking.

You can't drive Ferraris and Lamborghinis on a gravel road; you need to build the highway first, so the same logic applies to the world of finance. You can't have multi-billion-dollar hedge funds and shadow banks with poor

underlying infrastructure and regulation. We can agree that these institutions are beneficial to society regarding price discovery channels in the free market; however, disproportionate societal resources are wasted in that regard, which could be spread in the other sectors of the economy. Yes, we need hedge funds, since they're the ones that can discover the true price of assets in the markets and tell us the emperor has no clothes from time to time. We also need market vigilantes, and we need some market players to short the market when CEOs act in a misguided manner, but all of it is only possible within a paradigm that should form over a long time under regulative authorities.

In late-stage capitalism, when finance replaces the real economy, higher prices incentivize market players to bet for even higher prices, and lower prices also bring lower prices due to fear amongst traders and market speculators. A baby boomer in Vancouver told me that through the years he'd accumulated over three million dollars in his house as an investment vehicle. I told him that he was right to consider the world of finance and its endless miracles; however, the basic supply and demand law of economy told me that a millennial with a bunch of student loans and poor job prospects could never buy his house, so baby boomers couldn't pass these assets to the next generations at these imaginary prices. This phenomenon can be observed in many economies in late-stage capitalism. The economy basically becomes a rent seeking real estate economy, and most of the growth in GDP comes from growth in paper wealth of home owners until the housing market crashes, and it's hard to pick up the pieces at that time.

Late-stage capitalism is usually accompanied by fiat money in contrast to early stages. Although the currency of a mature economy might appreciate in global markets, it's very harmful for maintaining your export base, due to the high value of your currency. The so-called Dutch disease exists when you grow your financial sector at the expense of losing your exports and de-industrialization.

The US used to have a gold-based system in the booming 1950s, until it was revoked in the 1970s due to accumulation of too much debt, which left no choice but to break the gold peg. Fiat currencies always rely on the military might of the issuer of that currency, commodities, and the size of that economy. As soon as the hegemonic military superiority of that power is challenged effectively by a new rising power, and as soon as other economic rivals can throw their weight around, the currency shows severe signs of deteriorating inflation, and interest rates rise drastically. This will bring even further risk of global conflicts between the rising power and the relatively declining hegemon.

In late-stage capitalism, the citizens might receive a higher income compared to their fellow citizens in the emerging economies; however, the cost of living in a post-industrial developed economy is much higher due to the capital-intensive nature of a mature economy, which brings higher expenses and taxation to the citizen. Purchasing power parity should always be considered when comparing the quality of life between different stages of capitalism as well as different countries.

The same concept should be considered when measuring the size of economies. I believe the size of an economy should be measured in hours of labour rather than dollars. What matters the most is labour, productivity, and creativity that takes place within that economy rather than the dollar term of its GDP, which has different relations to the underlying productivity in different geographical regions.

Late-stage capitalism is also the time of psychological burden for the majority of citizens due to the burden of un-payable debt. As credit dries up eventually, the value of debt outweighs the value of its collateral, so many citizens become debt slaves or peasants to the house or land. It's essential to mention that debt per se is not evil or negative. Debt can be a motivating factor for debt holders to work hard and strive to pay it back. Moderate debt can be a motivating factor, but the problem arises when debt reaches a level that can't be serviced in any conceivable manner. This is the time that debt becomes destructive, since it creates a sense of general despair and helplessness in society.

In late-stage capitalism, every aspect of life, even human relationships, is subject to cost-benefit analysis. For example, people have to make a decision about who to marry based on financial aspects rather than true love. If you're a debt-burdened person in your twenties or thirties, you can climb the social ladder by finding the best spouse to help you get out of debt and despair rather than looking for true human connections. Lots of mid-age people also abandon their elderly parents due to cost-benefit calculations, since they can't carry the burden of their expenses. If you believe that capitalism is a repetition of gloom, doom, and boom cycles over an eighty-year period, then doom is a good word for late-stage capitalism.

Late-stage capitalism can also be called creditism. People rely on credit to purchase properties, and as the consumer relies more and more on credit rather than capital for investments, they also add a home equity line of credit to their mortgages to have more spending power. Due to de-regulation, lending goes through the roof, and financial institutions and the shadow banking system function with very little supervision by the authorities. In late-stage capitalism, it's very hard to build up equity in your house due to an over-reliance on credit, using your house as piggy bank. In this phase, compounding works against the benefit of the overly indebted masses, dragging them further down that rabbit hole of debt dependency.

In late-stage capitalism, the number of financial institutions reaches its peak. For example, a financial institution that used to have only one hundred employees in its early stages now has fifteen thousand employees all around the world, or the number of banks rise from eighty to two thousand in a matter of a few decades. The number of billionaires also increases from one or two in early stages to thousands due to social inequality and class divide.

Skyscrapers and extravagant shopping malls have popped up everywhere, but it's just a sign of tremendous debt. Building these structures will create what's called the skyscraper curse. It will soon be realized that jobs aren't created by building skyscrapers; meaningful jobs are created by building farms, factories, schools, ports, dams, and bridges.

The overcapacity accompanied with these luxury shopping malls, hotels, resorts, and high-rise properties creates a supply monster that needs to be fed on day to day basis despite the persistent weak demand in the market. This glut further debilitates the market participants to service debt effectively and contributes to the vicious cycle of further rise of debt to income.

In late-stage capitalism, the economy reaches a point that some loans can be considered un-payable, since the borrower is fully aware that the interest on the loan can't possibly be serviced over the course of the loan, let alone paying back the principal. But new loans continue to be issued until a systemic shock is reached.

In late-stage capitalism, lenders have the greatest amount of paper wealth and assets, but it's evident that debt can't be paid back in real terms, so all that numeric wealth means nothing much in real terms. Due to the shortsightedness of lenders, and assuming that more lending always results in more economic activity in the economy, the lenders overreach optimal lending, to the point that the lender can't afford any default from the borrowers anymore. Both lender and borrower find themselves in a compromised position that doesn't enable them produce meaningful economic growth. Excessive lending results in over-indebtedness of governments, corporations, and households, which results in higher taxation and a more capital-intensive economic environment. This phenomenon further deters from productive investments, which leads to a vicious cycle of inadequate investments as well as tremendous slack in creating meaningful labour participation.

Mature economies can be observed by emerging economies, so they might do their best to avoid such a harsh destiny, but in reality, nothing much can be done. Compound growth does its job according to a simple mathematical equation. For example, all countries observed Japan when they matured in the late 1980s, but they've never been able to stop their own similar desperate fate.

At late-stage capitalism, systemic crisis happens, so the majority of market players and home owners find out that the value of their home equity line of credit plus their mortgage exceeds the value of their house or the collateral, so they can't sell the house and pay back the loan for a long time. This means that they have to carry the burden of paying back the mortgage without much gain in the equity built in their house. The borrower who is fatigued with debt over the years can't pay back or service the debt in real terms after inflation, which results in net loss for lenders in the end. Lenders might accumulate tremendous assets and wealth on paper, but the true value of those assets depends on the existence of healthy, productive, creative, and innovative workers who can produce value and pay back the loans in real terms.

In late-stage capitalism, financial institutions finally reach the bitter realization that the borrowers have been severely damaged by the ongoing weight of their debts, so they have lost the health, creativity, and productivity needed to pay back the loans in real terms. For example, the lender might possess a million-dollar loan, which looks very impressive as a measure of the lender's wealth, but the borrower is a single dad with a history of diabetes, obesity, mental health issues, and autoimmune disease. The borrower also doesn't have any significant savings. He's currently on sick leave due to some sort of work injury. It's evident that this person can't pay back the loan in real terms over the course of the loan, in contrast to the paper wealth of the lender who might wrongly consider this as a sound investment. In simple terms, the quality of issued loans is nothing more or less than the quality of people who borrowed.

As a matter of fact, the numeric wealth expressed by money is an abstract claim on the existing real wealth in the economy that relies on productive workers in order to create real goods and services.

So the real wealth of a society can only be observed and measured in terms of the existence of a healthy population who is motivated to create value.

In late-stage capitalism, compromised borrowers result in compromised lenders, which brings the whole system down into a severe and abrupt decline. Both borrower and lender are suffering due to this mathematical equation called compounding. Lenders who have assets on paper realize that other economies in early or mid-stage capitalism get ahead and leapfrog to surpass the mature economy. They steal the torch from the mature economies by building mega-ports, mega-bridges, and large dams, while the mature economies can't even fix the roads or upgrade their own infrastructure, despite massive paper wealth. Therefore, the lenders who have wealth on paper soon realize that they have created a capital-intensive, mature economy that lacks infrastructure, creativity, and productivity.

In late-stage capitalism, people might blame a piece of legislation for all of our wrongdoings and misfortune; for example, it can be said that had we stayed away from merging commercial and investment banks, we would never have had such bad outcome. Or they might say the bloody elite are the source of all problems, and so on and so forth. This notion is just an innocent and childish rejection of the core fact that compound growth and the mathematical equation of exponential functions are inherent in capitalism, and bust cycles happen regardless of the previous actions of the elite. These cycles are unavoidable and inherent in capitalism.

At that stage, there are multiple societal conflicts at different layers of society. A severely debt-burdened society expresses tension at every level in late-stage capitalism. Tensions can arise between the elderly and the youth over how much tax the working members of the society should pay in order to maintain pensions for the retirees. Tensions can arise between the rich and the poor. The poor blame the rich for their monopoly and opportunistic behaviour, while the rich blame the poor for their stupidity and shortsightedness. Tensions can arise between classes; for example, people can blame the billionaire class for the misfortune of the poor. Tensions can arise between different political parties that move toward extreme sides of the spectrum in late-stage capitalism. Both right and left shift toward two extreme, opposing views, representing a divided community. Anytime you watch TV or connect to your social media page, you can view conflicts and heated debates about a newly realized problem.

Almost all of these tensions and conflicts are the result of ugly deleveraging that happens to millions of people in late-stage capitalism. Only a minority can go through a beautiful deleveraging and save their main assets through the bust cycle, and I am not solely talking about financial assets. An asset can be labour capital, skills, health, houses, savings at the bank, family, or even a kind friend. For example, a person might lose their skills and labour capital through long absence from work due to secular stagnation of wages, taxes, and inflation; another person might get diagnosed with lung cancer, since he or she smoked for years due to the high stress of living paycheque to paycheque.

In late-stage capitalism, multicultural societies also can have higher tensions via cultural clashes. Multiculturalism becomes harder to maintain as resources perish and the economy shows signs of fatigue, and it's instinctual for people to blame the others in tough times.

Despite the rise of tensions and hardship for the people, there's usually very little acceptance that the blame mainly lies with the ideology of capitalism and its inherent boom-and-bust cycles of compound growth. Societies look for simple solutions, as in late-stage capitalism the society is fatigued and unable to search for solutions, let alone implement good outcomes. Soon the average citizen is no longer able to both produce and consume in a meaningful way due to a sudden and abrupt credit shutdown, as well as a fatigued stagnant market. At this time, the economy effectively enters end stage capitalism which is typically accompanied with delinquencies and defaults.

In end-stage capitalism, there's a possibility that internal economic pressures can turn outward and create kinetic wars between separate countries and economic regions in the world.

All of a sudden, thousands of twenty-year-olds are shooting each other in the battlegrounds. War expands into a global conflict. Millions of people are affected around the world, supply chains are disrupted, food supplies perish globally, and innocent people suffer.

It's evident to me that our global community is repeating the old cycle again as I write this book, and that's the main reason I decided to write about it.

Chapter Six

Navigating into the Future and Solutions

We are at the stage where capitalism has been engraved in everybody's mind and soul for centuries, to the point that considering freedom from this paradigm is impossible. We live in a world where our only hope now is to reach a peaceful global financial reset and a beautiful global deleveraging.

Only a few minor regions in the world are benefiting from the early stages of capitalism. The major economies around the world, including China, the United States, Germany, France, Britain, Brazil, and Russia, are either in late-stage capitalism or are maturing into the late stage very soon. Global capitalism is no longer in its benevolent phase. The signs are evident. Debt saturation, financialization of economies, social inequality, central planning, protectionism, kinetic wars, asset bubbles, and a lack of global consensus amongst superpowers are signs that we are entering into a dangerous and dark phase in our collective global consciousness. Unfortunately, one can say that we can't abandon capitalism at this point without a huge loss of innocent human lives, since capitalism has created profoundly irreversible discrepancies that can't be undone without unbearable pain.

After studying the history of capitalism, it's evident to me that it can bring extremely joyful times of extravagance as well as horrendous crunches, depending on the credit cycle. We can't abandon these cycles, but we can wisely respond to them in order to reduce collateral damage, so the only remaining option is to learn from past history and aim for a new, peaceful global reset.

It's important to determine if we can start another cycle of prosperity without a conflict this time. Can we avoid repeating what happened in the last century? Can we empower our international institutions again to reach and achieve a united global consensus? This time, humanity needs to not evolve in technological terms and in the invention of military weapons. We don't want to reset through wars and the massive loss of innocent lives. We need to prevent the loss of each individual life. We need to prevent direct wars, starvation, malnutrition, and disease for billions of sacred lives in this universe and on this planet. We need to preserve every individual's integrity and sense of honour through a new sense of wisdom based solely on global sympathy for our fellow human beings.

The scary notion is that bust cycles of end-stage capitalism provide the most fertile ground for negative human traits to manifest themselves in the most brutal fashion. The rapid movement of masses from riches to rags through this rollercoaster can result in world wars. We need to learn from the past. We need to reach a stable new world order without massive casualties, death, and despair. Capitalism is no more than an accounting system; what scares me the most is when evil rises based on the mismatch of accounting and the underlying real wealth, as we witnessed eighty years ago. Today, I warn that the risk of loss of 500,000,000 innocent lives is a valid one and should be prevented at all costs.

A united global consciousness needs to evolve to adopt a new sense of wisdom and empathy toward one another in order to reach a new dimension in human collaboration and peace. The new dawn of opportunities, debt jubilee, global collaboration, worldwide sympathy, investing in transforming ourselves, and new technologies can bring a new heaven into this world while preserving the decency and dignity of every single sacred and precious human life on planet Earth.

This time the fish in the fish bowl needs to realize that the fish has a separate identity from the bowl. The true identity of the fish can only be manifested in the ocean.

Compound growth is not the master. It is just a mathematical equation.

REFERENCES

1) Richard C. Koo. (2022). Pursued Economy. Wiley.
2) Henry Hazlitt. (1988). Economics in One Lesson. Crown Currency.
3) Robert Z. Aliber, Charles P. Kindleberger (2023). Manias, Panics, and Crashes. Palgrave Macmillan.
4) Richard Vague. (2019). A Brief History of Doom. University of Pennsylvania Press.
5) Richard Vague. (2023). The Paradox Of Debt. University of Pennsylvania Press.
6) Steve Keen. (2011). Debunking Economics. Zed Books.
7) Ray Dalio. (2017). PRINCIPLES. Avid Reader Press/Simon and Schuster.
8) Ray Dalio. (2021). Principles for Dealing with the Changing World Order. Avid Reader/ Simon and Schuster.
9) Matthew C. Klein, Michael Pettis. (2021). Trade Wars Are Class Wars. Yale University Press.
10) Olivier Blanchard, Lawrence H. Summers. (2019). Evolution Or Revolution?. The MIT Press.
11) David Graeber. (2014). Debt: The First 5000 Years. Melville House.
12) Carmen M. Reinhart, Kenneth S. Rogoff. (2011). This Time Is Different. Princeton University Press.
13) Remarks by Governor Ben S. Bernanke. (2004). The Great Moderation. Eastern Economic Association. federalreserve.gov/boarddocs/speeches/2004/20040220/
14) Charles Goodhart, Manoj Pradhan. The Great Demographic Reversal. (2020). Palgrave Macmillan.
15) Mark Thornton. (2018). The Skyscraper Curse. Ludwig von Mises Institute.

www.ingramcontent.com/pod-product-compliance
Lightning Source LLC
LaVergne TN
LVHW081525060526
838200LV00044B/1998